Bohemian-inspired

JEWELRY

50 DESIGNS USING LEATHER, RIBBON, AND CORDS

LORELEI EURTO & ERIN SIEGEL

INTERWEAVE.
interweave.com

EDITOR: Michelle Mach

DESIGNER: Karla Baker

ART DIRECTOR: Liz Quan

PHOTOGRAPHY: Joe Coca

ILLUSTRATIONS + PHOTO STYLING:
Ann Swanson

PRODUCTION: Katherine Jackson

Interweave Press LLC
201 East Fourth Street
Loveland, CO 80537
interweave.com

Printed in China by C&C Offset.

Library of Congress
Cataloging-in-Publication Data

Eurto, Lorelei.
  Bohemian-inspired jewelry : 50 designs
using leather, ribbon, and cords
/ Lorelei Eurto, Erin Siegel.
     pages cm
  Includes bibliographical references
and index.
  ISBN 978-1-59668-498-0 (pbk.)
1. Jewelry making. 2. Textile jewelry.
3. Leatherwork. I. Siegel, Erin. II. Title.
  TT212.E98 2012
  745.594'2--dc23

                    2012001562

10 9 8 7 6 5 4 3 2 1

DEDICATED TO...

My love, Joe.   – LORELEI   My beautiful daughter, Nora.   – ERIN

ACKNOWLEDGMENTS

Our book could not have been written and published without the help of many wonderful people. We thank our three contributing designers, Mary Jane Dodd, Denise Yezbak Moore, and Tracy Statler for the time, energy, and great talents they put into their projects.

Thank you to our amazing editor, Michelle Mach. We really appreciate all the Saturday mornings she spent with us going over every detail. The guidance and knowledge she provided enhanced every aspect of this book. She went above and beyond what we could have hoped for. Thank you to Karla Baker, Liz Quan, Joe Coca, Ann Swanson, Katherine Jackson, Marlene Blessing, and the rest of the Interweave staff who made this book possible. Thank you to Acquisitions Editor Allison Korleski for believing in us and our book idea. Thank you to the bead suppliers who donated materials for the projects in this book: Artbeads.com, Bello Modo, Fusion Beads, Green Girl Studios, Marsha Neal Studio, Ornamentea, and Patina Queen.

A special thank-you goes out to the ceramic bead artists of the Beads-Of-Clay group for generously donating their art beads and pendants for the projects in this book. Also, a big thank-you to Marsha Minutella for sharing with us her expertise on silk ribbon care. Last, but not least, we'd like to thank the readers of this book and all our friends in the beading community. Thank you for your support!

ERIN & LORELEI

Thank you to my supportive husband, Joe, who stands by me and cheers me on in every creative endeavor I tackle. Thank you to my mother for listening to my ideas and giving support when I need it; to my father for always asking how the book was going and wanting all the details; to my sister for her willingness to test out jewelry designs or help me with color combinations; and to my brother for his love and support. Also, a huge thank-you to my coauthor Erin Siegel for approaching me about this collaboration and making this one of the most fun experiences in my beading career.   LORELEI

Thank you to my husband, Josh, for his love and enthusiastic support of my creative path no matter where it takes me. Thank you to The Riverwalk Bead Shop and Gallery for being the garden where my jewelry-making career blossomed. Thank you to Jon and Nancy Siegel for all their help and support throughout the entire book process. Thank you to my coauthor, Lorelei. Without her this book would still be an idea. I could not have realized this dream alone.   ERIN

CONTENTS

PROJECTS

INTRODUCTION

WHAT IS BOHEMIAN-INSPIRED JEWELRY?

It's an artistic, nature-inspired, and playful combination of materials and textures. A bohemian ensemble might include a floral-print dress, wood-soled sandals, a handmade leather bag, and a solid-color cardigan. In a similar way, a bohemian necklace might feature printed fabric ribbon, wood beads, and a handmade ceramic focal piece as in Batik Boutique by Lorelei Eurto (see p. 96). Key features of bohemian style include vibrant colors; organic materials such as wood, stone, or clay; and patterned or textured fibers such as leather, ribbon, or cord.

A few years ago, we both started adding leather, ribbons, and cords to our jewelry designs to set them apart in the crowded sea of bead and wire jewelry. Today, the contrast of soft fibers against beads and metal continues to captivate us. Ribbon and cord instantly add color, texture, and interest to any design. You can make an entire piece of jewelry with cord or just use it as an accent. You can also use it to set the mood and tone of a design. Leather, suede, linen, and cotton lend a casual feel, as shown by Awakening Lotus by Mary Jane Dodd (see p. 66), while silk ribbons add softness and elegance, as Nouvelle by Denise Yezbak Moore demonstrates (see p. 56).

When we first began making jewelry with fibers, we couldn't find any books on the topic. In writing this one, we've tried to address the questions we had as beginners, as well as share the helpful tips and tricks that we've discovered along the way. If you've been apprehensive about using silk ribbons in your jewelry because you're unsure how to care for them, you'll find the answers to all your questions in How to Care for Silk Ribbons (see p. 11). Or maybe you've always felt a little lost when it comes to finishing off the ends of ribbon or cord. Our book will introduce you to all the right types of findings to finish off your jewelry, plus show you how to use wire wrapping and knotting to attach cords to clasps. We'll even show you how to turn buttons into unique closures. With detailed sections on materials, findings, tools, and techniques, you can feel confident diving right in.

Years after our first jewelry creations, we still find ribbons, cords, and leather irresistible. We hope our fifty jewelry designs inspire you to create hundreds of your own.

LORELEI & ERIN

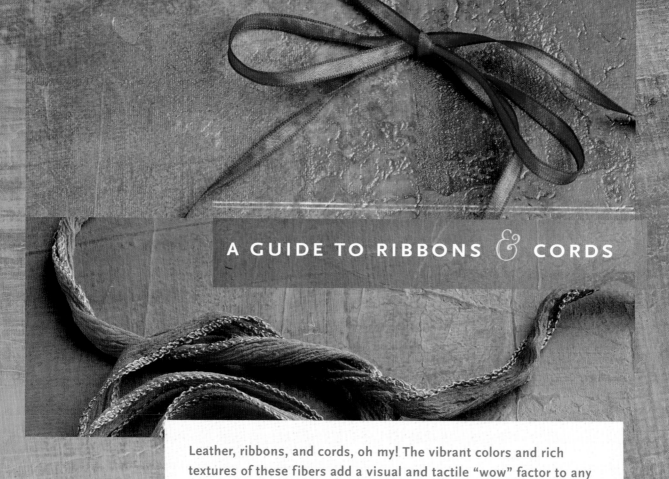

A GUIDE TO RIBBONS & CORDS

Leather, ribbons, and cords, oh my! The vibrant colors and rich textures of these fibers add a visual and tactile "wow" factor to any jewelry creation. Jump-start your imagination with more than twenty types of ribbons and cords available today.

SILK RIBBON works well paired with beaded strands or threaded through chain. Soft and comfortable against the skin, this ¾-inch opaque ribbon has stitched edges and deeper colors than the 2mm silk strands or fairy silk ribbons.

FAIRY SILK RIBBON is sheer with a wrinkled texture and handstitched edges. Delicate and lightweight, it gives jewelry designs an airy, ethereal feel.

SATIN RIBBON comes in a huge range of widths and colors. Stitched edges prevent this smooth ribbon from fraying until cut.

RIBBON YARN is a popular novelty yarn for jewelry. Available in solid or variegated colors, it's great for multistrand pieces.

SARI SILK is a gorgeous opaque ribbon in rich hues. It's made from recycled scraps of old sari fabric with fraying edges that give jewelry a rustic bohemian feel.

> **HAND-DYED SILK RIBBON** contains two or more variegated colors. The 7/16-inch ribbon is a soft silk cut on the bias with unfinished ends that will feather over time, giving jewelry an organic look.

> **SILK STRANDS** typically come in 40- to 42-inch lengths, a generous amount for most beading projects. Use for knotting and stringing large-holed beads.

> **SILK BEADING CORD** (carded) comes in eight sizes (2–16), with the lowest number being the thinnest cord. For best results, use the largest size cord your beads will easily string onto. The built-in needle makes it easy to string pearls and other small-holed beads. Use knot cups to finish the ends.

^ **SATIN CORD** also called rattail, is a 2mm rayon shimmery cord available in more than forty standard colors. It can be braided, knotted, or used for stringing.

> **DOUPPIONI SILK RIBBON** is produced when the cocoons of two or more silkworms come into contact. The tangled silk threads create the silk's nubby texture.

HOW TO CARE FOR SILK RIBBON

You've seen those luscious color-drenched strands of hand-dyed silk at your local bead store or online. You want to use them in your jewelry designs, but something keeps holding you back. How do you clean the ribbon if it gets dirty? How can you ensure the ribbon will hold up in a jewelry design? We had those same questions, so we asked ceramic bead artist and jewelry designer Marsha Minutella of Marsha Neal Studio to share her expert tips.

Q: How do I clean silk ribbon if it gets dirty?

A: Handwash colorfast silk ribbon in lukewarm water with a mild detergent such as Ivory soap or baby shampoo. Rinse thoroughly and then pat dry with a soft towel. Do not wring out the ribbon, as that will wrinkle it. Instead, lay it flat or hang it to dry. Some silks are not colorfast and may bleed. If you're unsure about the dye, ask the seller. If she doesn't know, don't buy it or test it before using.

Q: How do I iron or remove wrinkles from silk ribbons before designing with them?

A: Dampen the silk with water and hang to dry. Leaving the ribbons in a steamy bathroom may also help get out slight wrinkles. A more stubborn wrinkle may require ironing. Use the low heat (silk) setting. If your iron has steam, use it; if not, a fine mist of water helps. Silk scorches easily, so keep the iron moving constantly. You can also use a protective cloth, such as a thin dishtowel, over the silk.

Q: How can I ensure the silk ribbon will last in a jewelry design?

A: Here are three tips to ensure the longevity of your jewelry: First, make sure no sharp or ragged edges rub against the silk. Bead holes, jump-ring edges, sharp spots on metal, glass and stones can all have rough spots. Use a bead reamer or jewelry file to smooth the irregular edges. To avoid creating excess dust, sand under water when appropriate. Second, avoid designing pieces with excess movement, especially rubbing the silk against a hard surface, as this will eventually break down the silk fibers. Consider tying a knot to hold the movable part in place or use an epoxy such as E6000 to glue the silk to a metal finding. If you are wire wrapping an end, dip the end of the silk that will be covered by wire in epoxy or another sealant. This gives the wire a harder surface to grab onto, instead of biting into the silk. Third, use Fray Check on any exposed cut ends of ribbon. This glue seals the silk fibers and prevents them from raveling.

Q: What's the best way to store silk ribbons? On a spool? In a box?

A: Ideally, store your silk ribbon in a cool dry place with air circulation, but away from direct sunlight, high humidity, and extreme temperature changes. If you have one ribbon that you plan on using soon, wrap it loosely around your hand and place it in a mesh bag. If you have a bunch of ribbons, what I like to do is lay them over my hand, grab the middle of the ribbons, and tie one big, loose knot. When I need a ribbon, I pull it out without disturbing the rest. I like the idea of hanging the knot of ribbons on a smooth clothes hanger or shower curtain ring that can be moved around easily. For long-term storage, store ribbons flat.

Q: What's the best way to store finished jewelry made with silk ribbon? Hanging up? Laying flat?

A: It depends upon the amount of silk used, the jewelry design, and its weight. If your necklace has a simple wire-wrapped pendant on a ribbon, hanging the necklace is probably easiest. If your piece has some heft to it, laying it flat is better. As you work with and wear silk, you'll learn how best to store each piece.

PRINTED COTTON RIBBON gives your designs a fun, graphic appeal. Its sewn edges and tapered ends create a clean, finished look.

TRIMS typically used on furniture or drapes can give jewelry a one-of-a-kind look. Find this wonderful, but sometimes expensive, material at fabric stores.

EMBROIDERED RIBBON is a decorative ribbon with patterns woven onto it with thread. The wider varieties make great cuff-style bracelets.

VELVET RIBBON has a soft, luxurious feel. It adds elegance to jewelry designs.

EMBROIDERY FLOSS is a common sewing and stitching material made from cotton, rayon, linen, or metallic threads. Comprised of several strands twisted into a single thread, it's perfect for embellishment. It's available in more than 400 colors.

ORGANZA RIBBON is made of sheer nylon. Its beautiful sheen gives jewelry a dressy look.

CREPE CORD is a silk floral-patterned 6mm cord filled with yarn. Imported from Japan, this cord adds a feminine touch to jewelry.

LINEN CORD is a fine multistrand twisted cord with a waxy finish. Its texture makes it ideal for knotting, as the knots do not require glue for stability. It's available in different plies from 2 to 12, with the highest number being the thickest. It may be purchased by the yard or spool. Irish waxed linen cord from Belfast, Ireland, is the highest quality cord available.

WAXED COTTON CORD (not pictured) is available in larger sizes than linen cord and is not as waxy. Popular for creating sliding and overhand knots, cotton cord also works well for stringing beads with larger holes.

LACE TRIM can be hand-dyed in custom colors or left in its original state, either pristine white or an aged yellow. It's perfect for vintage-inspired designs.

ROUND LEATHER CORD is an inexpensive material that's popular for knotting. Greek leather is the highest quality.

LEATHER LACE is a rectangular strip of leather with a smooth surface on one or both sides. It's widely available in neutral colors and adds a casual look to designs.

HEMP is an inexpensive natural material. Popular in 1970s macramé jewelry, it's making a comeback as a fun and "green" alternative.

SUEDE LACE is a flat rectangular strip of leather that's finished with a fine velvetlike napped surface on both sides. This soft, supple material feels comfortable when worn and adds a rustic texture to designs.

RUBBER CORD is available as tubing (hollow) or cording (solid). This fun cord, commonly available in black, knots well and looks great in simple stringing designs.

CORD & RIBBON SPECIALTY FINDINGS

While we've suggested specific types of ribbons and cords to use with these specialty findings, once you start making jewelry, you may discover other options that fit your jewelry style. See the Techniques section (page 22) to learn how to use these specialty findings, as well as how to use standard jewelry findings such as bead cones and simple techniques such as knotting or wirework to finish your cord and ribbon jewelry.

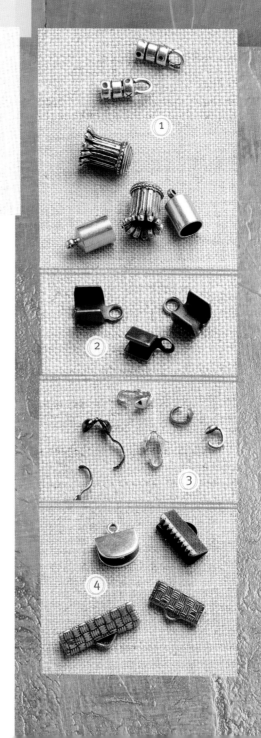

1. **CRIMP CORD ENDS** (also known as crimp end caps) are barrel-shaped tubes with a loop at one end. Insert round cord such as leather, cotton, satin, or rubber, and flatten with flat- or chain-nose pliers. **CORD ENDS** (also called end caps or bell caps) only require glue to secure.

2. **FOLD-OVER CORD ENDS** have three sides, one loop at the top, and a sharp point at the bottom to secure the cord. Use them with any flat rectangular cord such as leather or suede lace or narrow ribbons. Insert the ribbon or cord into the center and fold the left and right sides one at a time over the center using flat- or chain-nose pliers.

3. **KNOT CUPS** (also called clamshells or bead tips) are shaped like clamshells with either a single loop or double loops on one side and a stringing hole through the bottom. They're a perfect way to finish off silk beading cord or waxed linen cord. The clamshell covers the knot, giving your jewelry a more finished look.

4. **RIBBON ENDS** (also called ribbon crimp ends) offer a clean and simple way to finish fiber designs. Use them with any ribbon or trim. Match the width of the ribbon ends to the width of the ribbon. To use, insert the ribbon between the teeth of the open end and flatten with flat- or chain-nose pliers.

BASIC FINDINGS & MATERIALS

Having a selection of these items on hand allows you to make jewelry whenever inspiration strikes.

1. **BEAD CONES** typically cover the ends of a multistrand design, while **BEAD CAPS** are usually strung above and below round beads. Choose bead caps that match your bead size. For example, use 8mm bead caps with 8mm rounds.

2. **BEADING WIRE** is a flexible coated steel wire that comes in many colors and ranges in size from .012 to .021. Use a stronger, thicker wire (.018 to .021) for heavy beads and a thinner wire (.012 to .016) for lighter or small-holed beads such as pearls. Use crimping beads or tubes plus crimping pliers to finish the ends of your beading wire. **GAUGED METAL WIRE** comes in brass, silver, gold-filled, copper, and steel. To add more color to your design, choose non-tarnish coated copper craft wire. Sizes range from 12- to 34-gauge. The lower the gauge number, the thicker the wire.

3. **BEADS** are typically small pierced objects made of wood, shell, clay, glass, metal, stone, pearls, or plastic. **SPACERS** are used as decorative accents and strung just like beads.

4. **CHAIN** is a series of connected links typically made of metal. Using unsoldered chain allows you open and close the links like jump rings instead of cutting them, reducing waste and saving you money.

5. **CHARMS** are small round or flat components with either a loop or hole at the top. **PENDANTS** are larger, with a similar loop or hole. You can design an entire piece of jewelry around a pendant, drawing inspiration from the colors, shape, or material.

CLASPS

1. **HOOK-AND-EYE CLASPS** have two parts: a curved hook and a loop or ring.

2. **LOBSTER CLASPS** have springform levers that open and close. Swivel lobster clasps work the same way but have a rotating base that prevents jewelry from becoming twisted.

3. **S-CLASPS** are formed in an elongated S-shape and have soldered rings on each end.

4. **TOGGLE CLASPS** have a ring on one side and a bar on the other. The bar fits into the ring and, when pulled taut, prevents the clasp from coming apart.

5. **CRIMP BEADS** and **CRIMP TUBES** are used to finish a necklace or bracelet design by creating a loop to attach to the clasp. **CRIMP COVERS** wrap around a crimped bead or tube. When closed, they look like a round bead, giving your design a finished look.

6. **EAR WIRES** come in a range of metals and shapes. Popular types include french hook, kidney, and hoops.

7. **FILIGREE** resembles fine ornamental metalwork. It can be bent around beads or components or used as links.

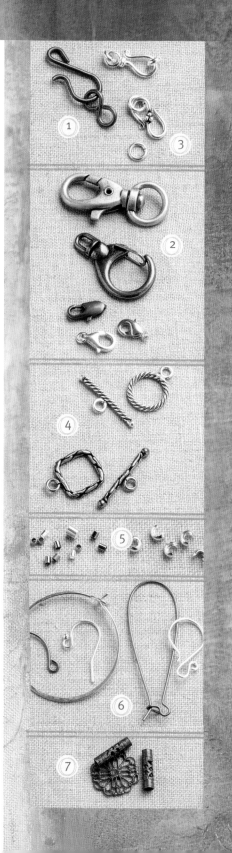

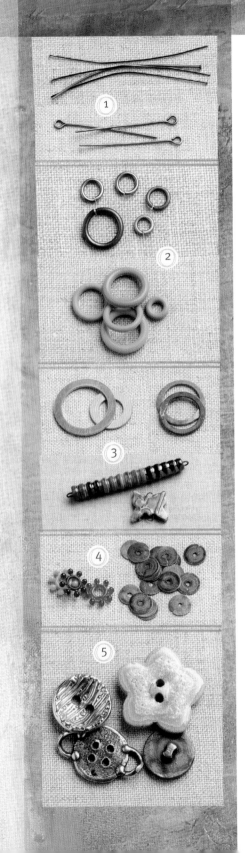

(1) **HEAD PINS** are sections of straight gauged wire with a flat nail head or round ball at one end, while **EYE PINS** have a simple loop at one end. Both are used to make beaded dangles with either simple or wrapped loops.

(2) **JUMP RINGS** are circular gauged wire rings that are either unsoldered (open) or soldered (closed). Soldered rings are great to use with an S-style or hook clasp, as they will not accidentally come apart. Rubber O-rings can be used in place of metal jump rings to add whimsy and color.

(3) **LINKS** (also called connectors) are beading components with a hole on each end or side. Use the holes to attach other links, findings, or wire. **METAL RINGS** created with heavy-gauge wire can be textured, hammered, or polished. **WASHERS** were originally intended for use with threaded screws. Hammer them and link them together with wire and jump rings.

(4) **PIXIES + SEQUINS** are vintage jewelry components that were popular in 1950–1970s costume jewelry. Pixies, with their small sunburst shape and balls on the ends of the spokes, pack a big punch when stacked. Sequins, found at crafting stores or antique shops, are small shiny or matte discs once used for decorative accents on costumes or clothing. String them like beads.

(5) **BUTTONS**, typically considered a sewing component, make great clasps. A shank button with a loop underneath makes a great closure, while buttons with 2 or 4 holes can be used as links, closures, or embellishments.

BASIC STRINGING TOOLS

With a good set of tools, you might feel like the jewelry practically makes itself! You'll want to spend some money on quality wire cutters and scissors. Sharp cutting tools make all the difference. There's nothing more frustrating than having wire cutters that fray the end of your beading wire (been there) or struggling with dull scissors to cut through ribbon or cord (done that). In this section, you'll find both common and not-so-common jewelry-making tools that will help you confidently craft the projects in this book and beyond.

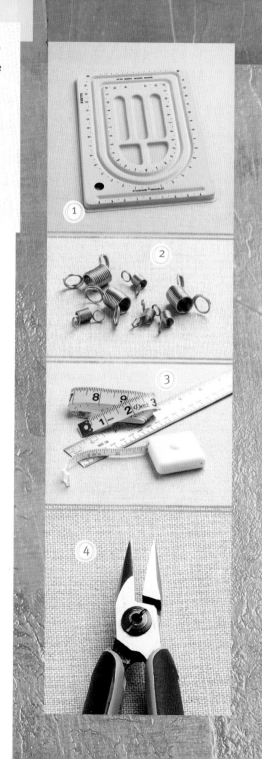

1   **BEAD BOARDS** are flocked plastic trays with grooves or channels on which to arrange beads for necklaces or bracelets before stringing them on beading wire. While measurements along the inside and outside of the grooves give you a general idea of length, we recommend using a ruler or measuring tape for final measurements.

2   **BEAD STOPS** are metal springs with a coil on each end that prevents beads from sliding off the end of your beading wire while you work. No more crying over spilled beads! Use two or more stoppers to work on multiple stands or check the length of an unfinished necklace. Bead stops also make it easier to place knots on a specific spot on a cord.

3   **RULERS AND MEASURING TAPES** measure wire, cord, and ribbon, as well as your in-progress and finished pieces. Metal rulers measuring 18" are especially handy, since that's a common necklace length. For measuring longer lengths, use a measuring tape. Flexible measuring tapes also work well for accurate wrist measurements, since they easily wrap around the wrist.

4   **CHAIN-NOSE PLIERS** have tapered jaws with a smooth, flat surface on the inside, making them ideal for use in small, tight spaces. The most versatile of the pliers, you can use them for a variety of tasks such as making sharp right-angle bends in wire, gripping wire or loops while wrapping, tucking wire ends in, opening and closing loops, and crimping or

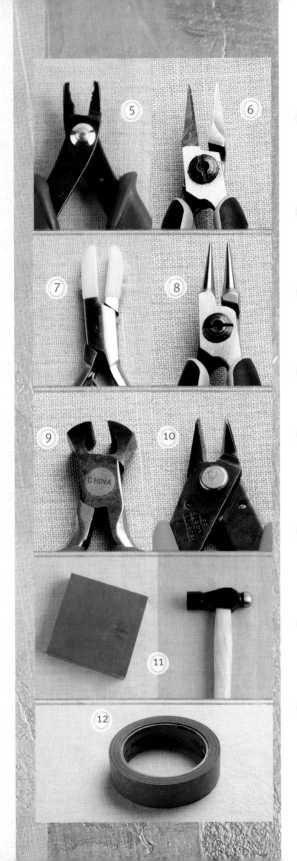

bending cord-end findings. Two pairs of chain-nose pliers are best for opening and closing jump rings.

5 **CRIMPING PLIERS** are used with crimp tubes to secure beading wire to a clasp. Crimping pliers come in three sizes: micro, regular (the most common size), and mighty. Crimping pliers are a must-have tool for creating professionally finished, secure connections.

6 **FLAT-NOSE PLIERS** have flat squared jaws of uniform (non-tapered) length. They are often used like chain-nose pliers. They're ideal for materials that require more surface area than chain-nose pliers such as large jump rings or thick wire gauges.

7 **NYLON-JAW PLIERS** are like flat-nose pliers, except their squared jaws are covered with a thick nylon coating. Use these pliers instead of flat-nose pliers when closing cord or ribbon-end findings to prevent marring the metal.

8 **ROUND-NOSE PLIERS** with their smooth, round, tapered jaws create loops in wire. Make different-sized loops by bending the wire at different places along the jaws.

9 **SIDE CUTTERS OR FLUSH CUTTERS** with their concave inside jaws and flat outside jaws are used to cut gauged metal wire. If you are using side cutters, lay the flat side against your work to make a clean flush cut. Most standard cutters can snip 20-gauge or thinner wire but follow the manufacturer's recommendations.

10 **WIRE CUTTERS OR NIPPERS** are designed solely to cut flexible beading wire cleanly with their sharp, thin, narrow blades. Using them to cut gauged wire ruins the blades. Once marred, the blades will fray the ends of your beading wire and make it unsuitable for lasting jewelry.

11 **BENCH BLOCK AND BALL-PEEN HAMMER** are used together to work-harden wire to strengthen it. The bench block provides a hard flat surface to hammer on. The hammer has two sides, one for flattening and one for texturing.

12 **PAINTER'S TAPE** can be wrapped around your chain-nose pliers if you don't own nylon-jaw pliers. In some instances, this method works better than nylon-jaw pliers because chain-nose pliers allow for greater control in small spaces. Avoid substituting other types of tape, since they'll leave a sticky residue that's difficult to remove.

TOOLS FOR RIBBON, LEATHER & CORDS

1. **BIG EYE BEADING NEEDLES** are flexible twisted needles with a large collapsible eye that allows beads to fit over it for stringing. While they're commonly used to string beads onto silk beading cord, they could easily be used to string beads onto wider materials such as ribbon.

2. **FRAY CHECK** or fabric fray sealant prevents material from fraying and raveling. Apply it thinly to cut edges and let it dry completely before handling your jewelry piece again.

3. **GLUES AND ADHESIVES** help ensure your jewelry lasts. Read the package labels for proper use and safety, as some contain toxic materials. With its pinpoint applicator, G-S Hypo Fabric Cement is perfect for sealing knots. Use instant adhesives to glue cord ends or other metal findings to cords and ribbons. Nontoxic fabric glue is a good choice for porous cords such as silk, cotton, and satin, although it takes slightly longer to dry than other adhesives.

4. **KNOTTING TWEEZERS** look like regular tweezers, except for their extremely fine pointed tips. Handle them with care, as the points can be very sharp. Knotting tweezers are essential for placing tiny knots, making them indispensable tools for jewelry made with silk beading cord.

5. **LEATHER PUNCHES** create small holes in leather or suede lace that can be used to attach jump rings or stringing materials. Leather punches come in two styles: one with a dial for multiple sizes or single-size hole punch.

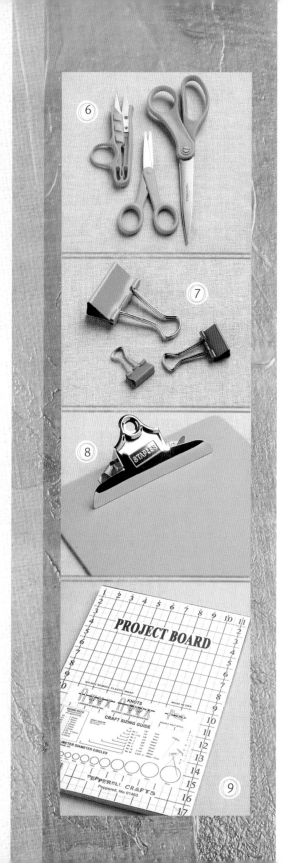

(6) **SCISSORS** with sharp blades make clean cuts. Use large shears for cutting thick cords and ribbons and multiple strands. Fine-tip scissors (small scissors with short, narrow blades) work best for cutting thin, fine cord and trimming threads. Their compact size helps prevent accidental cuts in the wrong place. Thread snips make quick, precise cuts, so they're perfect for trimming cords close to wire wraps or after a knot.

(7) **BINDER CLIPS**, easily found at office supply stores, hold cords together while you work. Choose small clips for single thin cords and large clips for thick cords or multiples.

(8) **CLIPBOARDS**, an office staple, make inexpensive alternatives to a macramé board and T-pins. Use the clip at the top to hold your work securely while knotting or braiding. Use a legal-sized board for a larger work surface.

(9) **MACRAMÉ BOARD** and **T-PINS** are handy tools for knotting and braiding. Mounting your jewelry project to a macramé board with sturdy T-pins helps you to maintain even tension. The top horizontal bar of the "T" prevents the project from slipping off and also makes the pins easy to move. The thick fiberboard may be stuck with pins multiple times. The board features a printed sheet with a grid and measurements. Some also include basic knot illustrations.

TECHNIQUES

This section will teach you the skills needed to make all the projects in this book. Most projects combine two or more techniques, giving the finished jewelry added interest and dimension. Please refer to the metric conversion chart on page 125 as needed.

STRINGING AND CRIMPING

Stringing

The most basic jewelry-making technique, stringing is the process of adding beads, one by one, to flexible beading wire or cord.

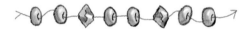

Crimping

Crimping uses flexible beading wire, crimp tubes, and crimping pliers to secure a clasp or other finding to a strand of strung beads. String the crimp tube and one half of the clasp onto the beading wire. Pass back through the tube, leaving a short tail. Lay the tube in the U-shaped back notch and squeeze the pliers, keeping the wires apart. Turn the tube 90° and place it inside the oval-shaped front notch. Squeeze the pliers, folding the tube in half. Continue turning the tube and squeezing the pliers to ensure a secure crimp. If possible, pass the tail back through the last bead.

Trim the tail close to the bead. Otherwise, trim the wire close to the crimp tube.

Alternatively, you can use crimp beads to crimp. Instead of using crimping pliers, crimp beads are secured by squeezing them flat with a pair of flat- or chain-nose pliers.

Using Crimp Covers

Place a crimp cover in the front oval-shaped notch of the crimping pliers. Insert the crimped tube into the crimp cover. Gently squeeze the pliers. Rotate the crimp cover and squeeze again. Repeat until the crimp cover is completely closed, with no overlapping edges.

WIREWORK

Using Jump Rings

Use a pair of chain-nose pliers to grasp each side of the split or break in the jump ring. Cover as much of the ring as possible with the pliers to preserve the jump ring's shape. Move one side toward you and the other away from you in a back-and-forth twisting motion. Never pull the ring apart to the sides, as this distorts its circular shape. To close, reverse the earlier motion. Move the ends just past each other and back for a tight closure.

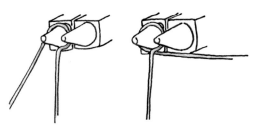

Making Simple Loops

Hold a pair of chain-nose pliers ¾ inch from the end of the wire. Bend the wire over the top of the pliers with your thumb to make a 90° bend. Position the round-nose pliers vertically inside the bend. Use your fingers to bend the wire up over the top jaw of the pliers and down. Reposition the wire into the bottom jaw of the pliers and bring the wire around the bottom jaw to complete the loop. Trim the wire inside the loop as close to the bend as possible.

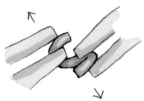

Making Wrapped Loops

Hold a pair of chain-nose pliers 1 inch from the end of the wire. Make a simple loop but do not trim the tail. In one hand, hold the loop with chain-nose pliers to preserve the loop shape. With the other hand, wrap the wire tail snugly down the shaft of the wire two to three times. Trim the tail as close to the wraps as possible. If needed, use the chain-nose pliers to gently squeeze the trimmed wire end to tuck it in and smooth any bur that might be left after snipping the wire.

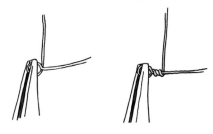

Making Double-Wrapped Loops

Hold a pair of chain-nose pliers 2 inches from the end of the wire. Make a wrapped loop but do not trim the tail. Wrap the wire back up over the previous wraps until you reach the loop. Trim the tail. A double-wrapped loop may be substituted for any wrapped loop.

Making Wrapped-Loop Dangles and Links

To make a dangle, string beads on a head pin. Use the chain-nose pliers to form a wrapped loop above the last bead.

To create beaded links, make a wrapped loop with a piece of wire. String the beads and form a wrapped loop.

To create a chain of beaded links, make a wrapped loop with a piece of wire, string the beads, and form another wrapped loop. Use another piece of wire to begin a wrapped loop, but before wrapping, attach the simple loop to the previous wrapped loop. Finish wrapping the loop, string the beads, and form another wrapped loop.

Making Wrapped-Loop Bails

Use 6 inches of wire to string a top-drilled bead 2 inches from the end. Bring each end of the wire up to the tip of the bead and cross the wires just above the bead. Using chain-nose pliers, bend the longer wire straight up to the point where the wires cross. Bend the shorter wire down, so it's horizontal. The two wires should form a 90° angle. Wrap the shorter wire around the long wire two to three times. Trim the short wire. Bend the long wire 90° and make a wrapped loop. Wrap the wire over the previous wraps. For a double-wrapped loop bail, continue wrapping the wire up toward the top loop.

Making Double-Loop Wrapped Bails

Use this technique for larger, heavier pendants. Center a top-drilled pendant on 12 inches of 20-gauge wire and cross the wires at the top. Using chain-nose pliers, bend both wires straight up at the point where the wires cross. Use both wires to form a wrapped loop. For a thicker wrap, continue wrapping the wires until the desired thickness is achieved.

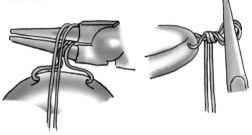

Making Wire-Wrapped Cord Ends Using Bead Cones

Hold the ribbon ¼ inch from the end. Hold 6 inches of 22-gauge wire parallel to the ribbon with half the wire extending past the short end of the ribbon. Using the other half of wire, bend the wire up onto itself. Begin to wrap the wire tightly around both the ribbon and the other half of the wire, moving toward the short end. Press the wire wraps with chain-nose pliers. If needed, trim excess ribbon. Use the free end of the wire to string 1 cone. Form a wrapped or double-wrapped loop.

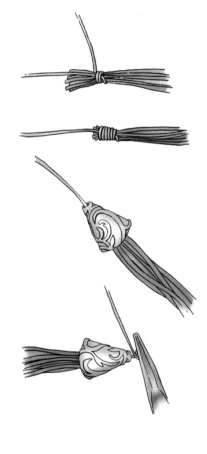

Making Wire-Wrapped Cord Ends

Use chain-nose pliers to hold the wire against the cord. With your other hand, wrap the wire tightly around the cord five to six times, making the wraps close together. Trim the wire ends. Use chain-nose pliers to tuck the wire ends in and press tightly to secure.

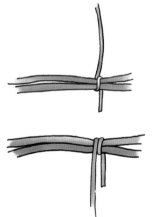

HAMMERING

Place your wire on a steel bench block. Use the flat end of a ball-peen hammer to flatten and work-harden the wire. Use the ball end of the hammer to texture the wire. Place a leather pillow or cloth under your bench block to dampen the sound of hammering and also to protect your work surface.

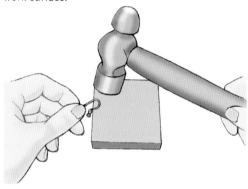

KNOTTING

Overhand Knot

This fundamental jewelry-making knot can be tied with one or more cords. Tie it in between beads or at the ends of cords. Make a loop. Pass the cord behind and then through the loop. Tighten.

For a double overhand knot, pass the cord through the loop a second time before pulling the knot tight.

Square Knot

Use this knot to tie two or more cords together. Pass the right cord over the left cord and through the loop. Tighten. Pass the left cord over the right cord and through the loop. Tighten.

Lark's Head Knot

This knot is typically used to attach cords to pendants. Fold the cord in half. String the folded end of the cord through the hole of the pendant. Pass the free ends of the cord through the loop. Tighten.

Half-Hitch Knot

This versatile knot looks complicated, but is very easy. It's used to make button or bead loops for closures, to embellish rings with beads, and to bind multiple cords together in a multistrand design. Start with an overhand knot or lark's head knot. Make a loop around the group of cords or the jewelry component (such as a ring). Pass the cord through the loop. Tighten.

Half-Hitch Knotted Loop

Tie a piece of cord at the base of the loop you are covering. Tie the cord on with an overhand knot, leaving a ½-inch tail parallel to the loop. Using the long end of cord, tie a half-hitch knot around the loop and the ½-inch tail. Pull tight. Make three more half-hitch knots around the loop and the tail. Trim the tail close to the last half-hitch knot. Continue to make half-hitch knots with the long cord until the entire loop is covered. Finish with a double overhand knot and pull tight against the last half-hitch knot. Trim the cord close to the knot.

To add beads to the half-hitch knotted loop, string a small bead (such as a seed bead) onto the cord before tying a half-hitch knot. Add beads to every other half-hitch knot as you go.

Slipknot

Use this knot to secure thinner cords such as waxed linen to a metal clasp. It can also be used to create an adjustable closure for necklaces and bracelets. Fold the cord back onto itself and make a loop around the cord. Bring the cord behind and then through the loop. Tighten.

Sliding or Slide Knot

This knot also works for creating adjustable closures for jewelry. Place the left and right cords parallel to one another with the ends in opposite directions. Fold one of the cords back onto itself about 3 inches. This is your working cord. Wrap the working cord around the other cord three times. Insert the working cord through the wraps, exiting the folded end. Tighten. Turn the necklace or bracelet over and repeat entire step for the other side.

Knotting with Tweezers

Knotting tweezers help place knots right where you want them to go. Make a loose overhand knot. Slide the tips of the open tweezers through the loop and and grip the cord where you want to place the knot. Pull the cord to tighten the knot. Slip the knot off the tweezers. If necessary, tighten the knot by pushing it with your fingers or the tweezers.

Braiding

Braids require three or more cords. You can add beads or dangles to braids for extra interest. Tie three cords (or three sets of cords) in a loose overhand knot. Pin the knot to a macramé board with a T-pin or clip to a clipboard. Separate the strands so you have left cord(s), middle cord(s), and right cord(s). Bring the left cord(s) over the middle cord(s). Bring the right cord(s) over the cord(s) now in the middle. Repeat entire step until you've reached the desired length. Hold the cords with consistent tension as you braid for even, professional work.

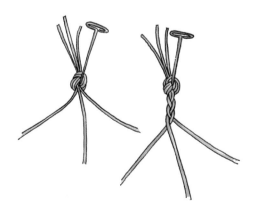

Crimp Cord Ends

Insert the end of the cord into the crimp cord end until the cord is close to the top. Position the cord end so that the loop is horizontal to the chain-nose pliers to prevent breakage. Use the pliers to flatten the center of the cord end, securing the cord.

Fold-Over Cord Ends

Place the end of the cord into the finding. Using flat- or chain-nose pliers, fold the left and right flaps down one at a time over the cord. Press firmly.

Knot Cups

Tie a double overhand knot at the end of the cord. Trim close to the knot. String the hole on the knot cup. Close the cup gently over the knot with the front notch of crimping pliers.

Ribbon Ends

Add a dab of glue to the end of the ribbon and insert it into the ribbon end. Squeeze the ribbon end closed with a pair of nylon-jaw pliers or flat- or chain-nose pliers wrapped in painter's tape to prevent marring the metal finding.

Leather Punch

Insert the leather or suede lace into the jaws of the punch. Squeeze the handles firmly until the tool has punched a clean hole in the lace.

PROJECTS

DAISY CUFF

LORELEI EURTO

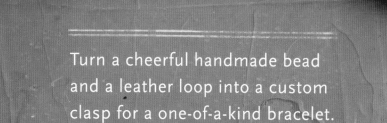

Turn a cheerful handmade bead
and a leather loop into a custom
clasp for a one-of-a-kind bracelet.

MATERIALS

1 green/yellow/orange 18mm ceramic daisy lentil

4 green/yellow/orange 30x10mm ceramic daisy 2-holed spacer bars

26 green 7mm rubber O-rings

18 brass 2mm spacers

25" of brown 3mm leather lace

TOOLS

Scissors

Ruler

TECHNIQUE

Overhand knot, page 26

FINISHED SIZE

6½" (adjustable to 8")

TIP

For easier stringing, cut the end of the leather lace at a diagonal.

1 Center the ceramic lentil on the leather lace. Use both strands to form an overhand knot. Snug the knot behind the lentil. Use 1 strand to string the left hole of 1 spacer bar, about ¼" from the previous knot. Use the other strand to string the right hole of the spacer bar.

2 Use 1 strand to form an overhand knot. String 1 O-ring, 1 spacer, and 1 O-ring; form an overhand knot. Repeat entire step with the other strand.

3 Use 1 strand to string the left hole of 1 spacer bar. Use the other strand to string the right hole of the spacer bar.

4 Repeat Steps 2–3 twice. Use 1 strand to form an overhand knot. String {1 O-ring and 1 spacer} six times. String 1 O-Ring. Repeat entire step with other strand.

5 Use both strands to form an overhand knot. Use both strands to form an overhand knot about 1" from the previous knot. For an adjustable bracelet, use both strands to form an overhand knot about 1½" from the previous knot. Otherwise, omit the previous knot and trim the leather ends to ¼".

DELICATE THINGS

ERIN SIEGEL

Create a unique decorative bail for a donut by making half-hitch knots with colorful silk beading cord and small copper beads.

MATERIALS

14 amethyst 6mm rounds

1 lavender-and-brown 28mm ceramic donut

31 antique copper 3mm faceted spacers

1 antique copper 21x10mm S-clasp with two attached 6mm soldered jump rings

2 copper 4mm knot cups

79" (1 card) of carnelian size 8 silk beading cord with attached needle

Fabric cement

TOOLS

Scissors

Ruler

Crimping pliers

Knotting tweezers

Bead stop (optional)

TECHNIQUES

Overhand knot, page 26

Double overhand knot, page 26

Lark's head knot, page 26

Half-hitch knot, page 26

Knot cups, page 28

FINISHED SIZE

16½"

TIP

To make evernly spaced knots, place a bead stop where you'd like to knot. Form the knot against the bead stop and move the bead stop to the next knot location.

1 Remove all the cord from the card. Stretch a small section. Repeat for entire cord.

2 Tie a double overhand knot at the end of the cord opposite the needle. Trim. Dab the knot with glue. Let dry. String 1 knot cup and close with crimping pliers. Attach the knot cup to one half of the clasp.

3 Tie an overhand knot. String 1 copper spacer and form an overhand knot. String 1 amethyst round and form an overhand knot. String 1 copper spacer and form an overhand knot.

4 Form an overhand knot about ½" from the previous knot. String 1 copper spacer and form an overhand knot. String 1 amethyst round and form an overhand knot. String 1 copper spacer and form an overhand knot. Repeat entire step five times.

5 Form a lark's head knot on the donut. Snug the lark's head knot against the last overhand knot. Working from left to right across the donut, form 2 half-hitch knots. *String 1 copper spacer and form 2 half-hitch knots.** Repeat from * to ** twice. Form 2 half-hitch knots. Repeat Steps 3–4. String a knot cup through the bottom; form a double overhand knot inside the knot cup. Trim. Dab with glue. Let dry. Close knot cup and attach to other half of the clasp.

VINTAGE GLAM

ERIN SIEGEL

MATERIALS

10 silver 7mm vintage metal sequins

8 antiqued brass 10mm washers

2 antiqued sterling silver ear wires

79" (1 card) of black size 8 silk beading cord with attached needle

TOOLS

Scissors

Ruler

Collapsible-eye beading needle

Knotting tweezers

Chain-nose pliers

TECHNIQUES

Overhand knots, page 26

Knotting with tweezers, page 27

FINISHED SIZE

3"

An unlikely combination of vintage silver sequins and ordinary brass washers make stunning earrings when woven flat with two silk cords.

TIP

Although these require only a few inches of cord, using the cord uncut allows you to keep the needle attached for future projects.

1 Fold the cord about 6" from the end opposite the attached needle. Use both cords to form an overhand knot, leaving a ⅛" loop.

2 Thread the collapsible-eye needle onto the cord so that you have a needle on each end. *Pass the attached needle through the hole of 1 sequin. Pass the collapsible-eye needle through the same hole in the opposite direction. Tighten the cord until the sequin sits below the previous overhand knot. Pass the attached needle through the hole of 1 washer. Pass the collapsible-eye needle through the same hole in the opposite direction. Tighten so that the sequin overlaps on top of the washer. Repeat from * four times, omitting the last washer. Use both cords to tie an overhand knot. Trim ends to ¼" and fray. Attach 1 wire ear wire to the cord loop created in Step 2.

3 Repeat Steps 1–2 for other earring.

LAVENDER

LORELEI EURTO

MATERIALS

2 pewter 20mm 2-holed buttons

2 brass 15x27mm ear wires

18" of purple 2mm silk cord

6" of brass 18-gauge wire

TOOLS

Bench block

Ball-peen hammer

Wire cutters

Sharpie pen or mandrel

Flat-nose pliers

TECHNIQUES

Hammering, page 26

Square knots, page 26

FINISHED SIZE

2¼"

Turn handmade buttons into unique earrings with a little silk cord and a piece of brass wire.

TIP

Hammering wire makes it stiff. This is called "work hardening," which helps the earrings hold their curved shape.

1 Bend the center of 3" of wire around a Sharpie pen, crossing the wire ends. Hammer the wire.

2 Leaving a 1½" tail, begin wrapping 9" of cord around one end of the crossed wires. Wrap the entire wire, slightly overlapping the wraps.

3 String the cord tail through 1 buttonhole. String the tail from Step 2 through the other buttonhole. Form a square knot. Trim ends to ¼." Attach 1 ear wire to the silk loop.

4 Repeat Steps 1–3 for second earring.

HOW DOES YOUR GARDEN GROW?

LORELEI EURTO

This earthy asymmetrical necklace
overflows with contrasting textures
from the smooth leather cord and
wood rounds to the faceted glass
and Lucite leaves.

MATERIALS

3 rust size 8° seed beads

108 matte metallic khaki iris 2.8mm drop seed beads

6 gold AB 12mm faceted rounds

1 green 20x25 ceramic "grow" oval

29 ebony 5mm wood rounds

3 burnt rust 23x13mm Lucite leaves

4 matte khaki 23x13mm Lucite leaves

3 yellow 11.5mm enameled flowers

4 brass 8mm filigree tubes

1 amber 40mm ceramic dragonfly pendant

1 pewter 20mm butterfly toggle clasp

4 brass 2" head pins

9 brass 4mm jump rings

1 brass 10mm etched jump ring

2 gunmetal 2mm crimp tubes

1 brass 9x5mm fold-over cord end

24" of brown leather cord

3" of brass 20-gauge wire

24" of .018 beading wire

TOOLS

Crimping pliers

Wire cutters

Round-nose pliers

2 pairs of chain- or flat-nose pliers

TECHNIQUES

Wrapped-loop bail, page 24

Overhand knots, page 26

Fold-over cord ends, page 28

Wrapped loops, page 23

FINISHED SIZE

Finished size: 20½"

1 Use the brass wire to string the pendant; form a wrapped-loop bail. Set aside. Use 1 head pin to string 1 rust seed bead on head pins and 1 enamel flower; form a wrapped loop. Repeat three times. Set aside. Attach one 4mm jump ring to 1 Lucite leaf. Repeat 5 times. Set aside.

2 Attach one 4mm jump ring to the ring half of the toggle. Center the previous jump ring on the leather cord. *

3 Use both cords to string 1 filigree tube. Use 1 cord to string 1 gold round. Use both cords to string 1 filigree tube and form an overhand knot.**

4 Repeat from * to ** twice. Use 1 cord to string 1 gold round. Use the other cord to string the "grow" bead (top to bottom). Use both cords to form an overhand knot. Use 1 cord to string 1 gold round and form an overhand knot. Repeat. Insert both cord ends in 1 fold-over cord end. Close. Use the etched jump ring to attach the cord end to the pendant.

5 Center the bar half of the toggle on the beading wire. Use both wires to string 1 crimp tube. Crimp.

6 Use 1 wire to string 6 drops. Repeat with other wire. Use both wires to string 2 wood rounds. Use 1 wire to string 10 drops. Repeat with other wire. Use both wires to string 3 wood rounds, 1 rust leaf, 1 flower dangle, 1 khaki leaf, and 3 wood rounds. Repeat entire step twice.

7 Use 1 wire to string 6 drops. Repeat with other wire. String 4 wood rounds, 1 khaki leaf, 1 flower dangle, and 1 wood round. Use 1 wire to string 2 drops. Repeat with other wire. Use both wires to string 1 crimp tube and one 4mm jump ring. Pass both wires through the crimp tube and crimp. Attach the previous jump ring to the etched jump ring.

AUTUMNAL ARRANGEMENT

LORELEI EURTO

Weaving cord through the lampwork discs, rather than stringing them, shows off more of the beads' colorful surface.

MATERIALS

1 brown 6mm etched raku lampwork rondelle

1 tan 6mm etched raku lampwork rondelle

6 assorted 18–22mm lampwork etched discs in purple, rust, and gold

5 assorted 14mm ceramic washers in crème brûlée, bronze, and aqua

20 rust 9mm plastic pixies

1 brass 7x14mm figure-eight link

2 copper 5mm daisy spacers

1 brass 7x14mm lobster clasp

2 brass 2" head pins

1 brass 4mm jump ring

13½" of brass 9.5x6.5mm unsoldered etched cable chain

16" of pale green 2mm silk cord

TOOLS

2 pairs of chain- or flat-nose pliers

Round-nose pliers

Scissors

TECHNIQUES

Overhand knots, page 26

Double-wrapped loops, page 23

FINISHED SIZE

22½"

TIP

To make an asymmetrical necklace feel cohesive, use some of the same beads on each side like the pixies used in this necklace.

1 Use the jump ring to attach the lobster clasp to one end of the chain. *Attach 1 pixie to link 4 of the chain, by opening and closing the chain link as you would a jump ring. Repeat from * nine times, adding pixies to links 9, 14, 19, 24, 29, 34, 39, 44, and 49.

2 Center the last chain link on the silk cord and form an overhand knot about ½" from the chain link.

3 Use 1 cord to string 1 disc. Use the other cord to string the disc in the opposite direction. Snug the disc against the knot. Use both cords to string 1 pixie, 1 washer, and 1 pixie. Repeat entire step four times.

4 Use 1 cord to string the remaining disc. Use the other cord to string the disc in the opposite direction. Use both cords to string the figure-eight link and form an overhand knot snug against the last disc. Trim.

5 Use 1 head pin to string 1 daisy spacer and 1 brown rondelle; form a double-wrapped loop that attaches to the same end of the figure-eight link as the cord. Repeat entire step using the tan rondelle.

RAKU RIBBONS

ERIN SIEGEL

Colorful ribbon yarn
mimics the shimmering
colors in the handmade
raku pendant.

MATERIALS

2 mauve 8mm ceramic rounds (A)

6 red 10mm raku ceramic beads (B)

2 gray 14mm crackle ceramic rounds (C)

2 red 13mm ceramic rounds (D)

1 metallic 45mm textured raku pendant

20 copper 6mm bead caps

2 copper 8x19mm cones

1 copper 17mm rope toggle clasp

12 copper 2.5" ball-end head pins

12 copper 5mm jump rings

6 multicolored 28" silk/cotton 7mm ribbon yarns

12" of copper 22-gauge wire

12" of copper 20-gauge wire

TOOLS

Wire cutters

2 pairs of chain- or flat-nose pliers

Round-nose pliers

Scissors

Ruler

TECHNIQUES

Cones with wire wrapping, page 25

Double-loop wrapped bail, page 25

Double-wrapped loops, page 23

Overhand knots, page 26

FINISHED SIZE

19"

1 Use the 20-gauge copper wire to string the pendant; form a double-loop wrapped bail. Set aside.

2 Use 1 head pin to string 1 bead cap, 1A, and 1 bead cap; make a double-wrapped loop that attaches to 1 jump ring. Repeat for a total of 2A. Use 1 head pin to string 1 bead cap, 1B, and 1 bead cap; make a double-wrapped loop that attaches to 1 jump ring. Repeat five times for a total of 6B. Use 1 head pin to string 1 bead cap and 1C; make a double-wrapped loop that attaches to 1 jump ring. Repeat for a total of 2C. Use 1 head pin to string 1 bead cap and 1D; make a double-wrapped loop that attaches to 1 jump ring. Repeat for a total of 2D. Set dangles aside.

3 Place the ends of six 28" ribbons parallel to the middle of 6" of 22-gauge wire. Adjust the ribbons so that they extend ¼" below the wire. Use one end of the wire to wrap the cord tightly toward the short ends of the ribbon. Use the other half of the wire to string 1 cone and form a double-wrapped loop that attaches to one half of the clasp.

4 Use all ribbons to form an overhand knot about 4" from the cone.

5 Use three ribbons to string 1A and 1B. *Use all 6 ribbons to form an overhand knot about 1" from the previous knot.** Use 3 ribbons to string 1B and 1C. Repeat from * to *. Use 3 ribbons to string 1B and 1D. Repeat from * to **.

6 Use 3 ribbons to string the pendant. Repeat Step 5, reversing the knotting and stringing sequence. Repeat Step 5 from * to **. Repeat Step 4 with the remaining cone and other half of the clasp.

ELEMENTS OF EARTH

ERIN SIEGEL

Create the look of beaded beads with the clever stringing technique used in this richly colored choker.

MATERIALS

7 g of copper-lined crystal clear size 11°
seed beads

60 blue crazy lace agate 6mm rounds

5 wood 25mm rounds

3 bronze 15x20mm raku pinch barrels

3 silver 15x20mm flat ovals

1 silver 25mm textured 2-holed button

33½' of dark chocolate 4-ply Irish waxed
linen cord

TOOLS

Scissors

Ruler

TECHNIQUES

Overhand knots, page 26

Half-hitch knots, page 26

Double overhand knots, page 26

Square knots, page 26

FINISHED SIZE

16½"

TIP

*Add seed beads to the knotted loop to create a fancier clasp
(page 26).*

1. Cut the cord into three 10¼' pieces and one 2' piece. Fold the three 10¼' cords in half and form an overhand knot at the folded end, creating a 1" loop.

2. Use the 2' cord to form an overhand knot below the previous knot, leaving a ½" tail. Use the long cord to form five half-hitch knots around the loop and the tail. Trim tail. Continue forming half-hitch knots until the loop is covered. Form a double overhand knot. Trim.

3. Use all 6 cords to string 1 raku barrel and form an overhand knot.

4. Use 1 cord to string 2 agate rounds. Repeat five times for the remaining 5 cords. Use all cords to form an overhand knot.

5. Use all 6 cords to string 1 wood round. *Use 1 cord to string 25 seed beads. Pass the cord back up through the round.** Repeat from * to ** with remaining 5 cords. Tighten cords. Use all 6 cords to form an overhand knot.

6. Use 2 cords to string 1 silver oval. Use all 6 cords to form an overhand knot.

7. Repeat Steps 4–5. Repeat Steps 3–6. Repeat Steps 4–5. Repeat Steps 3–6.

8. Divide cords in half. Use the two sets of cords to form three square knots. Use 3 cords to string 1 buttonhole and 3 cords to string the other buttonhole. Form a square knot. Trim.

OXFORD CIRCUS

LORELEI EURTO

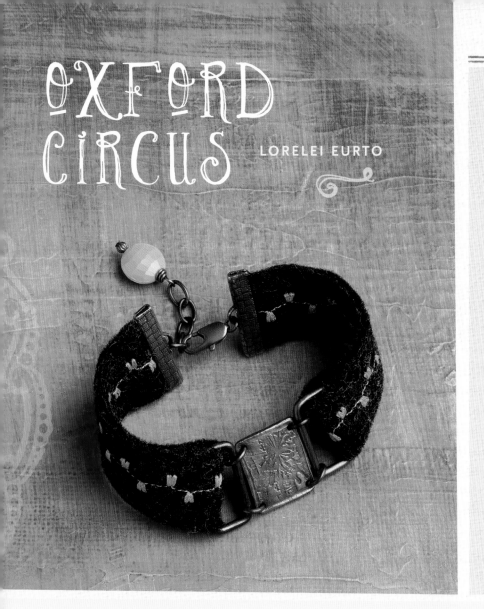

MATERIALS

1 aqua 12mm faceted Lucite coin

1 brass 2mm melon round

1 bronze 21x18mm 4-holed link

1 brass 8x12mm lobster clasp

1 brass 2" head pin

1 brass 4mm jump ring

4 brass 7mm jump rings

2 brass 12x24mm rectangular jump rings

2 brass 25mm ribbon ends

1¼" of brass 5x7mm unsoldered oval chain

12" of gray-and-aqua 1" embroidered wool ribbon

TOOLS

Scissors

2 pairs of chain- or flat-nose pliers

Round-nose pliers

TECHNIQUES

Ribbon ends, page 28

Wrapped loops, page 23

FINISHED SIZE

8–9"

This embroidered wool ribbon bracelet works up quickly, thanks to the similar widths of the ribbon, rectangular jump rings, and bronze link.

1 Center the rectangular jump ring on 6" of ribbon. Insert both ends of ribbon into the ribbon end. Close the ribbon end with chain-nose pliers.

2 Use the 4mm jump ring to attach the clasp to the ribbon end.

3 Use one 7mm jump ring to attach one hole of the connector to the rectangular jump ring. Repeat.

4 Repeat Steps 1 and 3 for the other half of the bracelet.

5 Attach one end of chain to the free ribbon end, opening and closing the chain link as you would a jump ring. Use the head pin to string the melon round and the Lucite coin; form a wrapped loop that attaches to the other end of the chain.

TRiPLe LOOP

ERIN SIEGEL

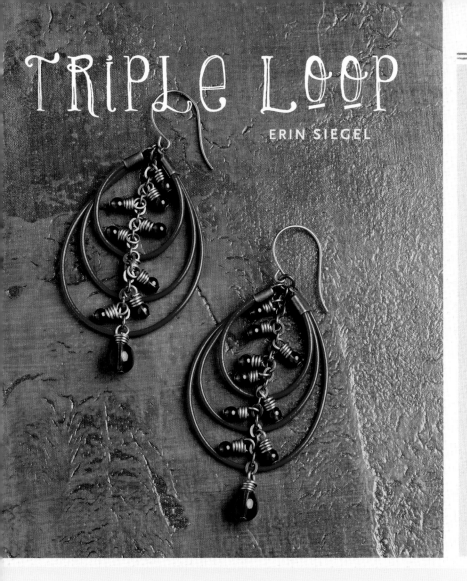

MATERIALS

2 amethyst 8mm glass rounds

18 amethyst 4mm rounds

20 antique brass 3" head pins

2 antique brass 4.75mm jump rings

2 antique brass ear wires

4 antique brass 9mm fold-over cord ends

4½" of antique brass 4x3.5mm flat cable chain

24" of red 1.5mm Greek leather cord

TOOLS

Wire cutters

2 pairs of chain- or flat-nose pliers

Round-nose pliers

Scissors

Tape (optional)

TECHNIQUES

Fold-over cord ends, page 28

Double wrapped loops, page 23

FINISHED SIZE

3½"

Bold loops of Greek leather and a bevy of beaded dangles make fashionable light-weight earrings.

TIP
Wrap your chain- or flat-nose pliers with painter's tape to prevent marring the cord ends.

1 Cut the leather into two 5" pieces, two 4" pieces, and two 3" pieces.

2 Place the ends of one 5" piece, one 4" piece, and one 3" piece into 1 cord end and close. Repeat for the other cord ends.

3 Use 1 head pin to string 1 amethyst round; form a double-wrapped loop that attaches to the second link of 2" of chain. Repeat eight times, attaching the dangles to every other chain link. Use 1 head pin to string 1 glass round; form a double-wrapped loop that attaches to the last chain link. Use 1 jump ring to attach 1 cord end, the free end of chain, and the other cord end to 1 ear wire.

4 Steps 2–3 for other earring.

TIDY TRIMMINGS

LORELEI EURTO

Use filigree links to create custom ribbon ends for a springtime bracelet.

MATERIALS

6 jade 5x8mm faceted rondelles

3 green 8mm sugared Lucite rounds

3 pink 8mm sugared Lucite rounds

4 faux brass 15mm Lucite rounds

1 pink 15mm Lucite round

2 brass 15mm princess-cut filigree links

1 brass 29x15mm S-hook clasp

2 brass 2" head pins

2 brass 10mm etched jump rings

2 copper 2mm crimp tubes

7" of pink-and-green 12mm wide trim

8" of copper .018 beading wire

Fabric glue

TOOLS

Metal hole punch

Crimping pliers

Wire cutters

Round-nose pliers

2 pairs of chain- or flat-nose pliers

TECHNIQUES

Wrapped loops, page 23

FINISHED SIZE

8¼"

TIP

Adding glue to the ends of the trim not only keeps it from raveling, but also makes it easier for the ribbon ends to firmly grasp the trim.

1 Apply fabric glue to the trim ends. Let dry.

2 Punch one 1.8mm hole in the center of 1 filigree. Bend filigree in half with flat-nose pliers, leaving space to insert trim. Use 1 head pin to string center hole; form a wrapped loop above the filigree fold. Insert one end of trim and close filigree. Repeat entire step for other end of trim. Set aside.

3 Use the beading wire to string 1 crimp tube and 1 etched jump ring. Pass back through the crimp tube and crimp.

4 String 1 green round, 1 jade rondelle, 1 pink round, 1 brass round, 1 jade, the pink 15mm round, 1 green round, 1 brass, 1 jade, 1 pink round, 1 jade, 1 brass, 1 green, 1 jade, 1 brass, 1 pink round, and 1 jade. Repeat Step 3.

5 Attach the jump ring and one side of the clasp to one end of the trim. Repeat for the other end of the bracelet.

QUIETUDE

LORELEI EURTO

A pretty button hides a plain hook
clasp in this sunny necklace filled
with lampwork discs.

let thy
words
be few

MATERIALS

2 mint/orange/ivory 10–12mm bumpy etched lampwork discs (A)

1 orange-and-white 12mm etched lampwork disc (B)

1 yellow 12mm etched lampwork disc (C)

1 orange 12mm etched lampwork disc (D)

1 yellow-and-orange 13mm etched lampwork disc (E)

1 cream 14mm etched etched lampwork disc (F)

1 orange-and-white 16mm bumpy etched lampwork disc (G)

3 mint-and-yellow 15–18mm etched etched lampwork discs (H)

1 cream-and-yellow 18mm etched lampwork disc (J)

1 tan-and-blue 15mm ceramic heart

1 antiqued silver 12mm flower shank button

1 pewter 45mm botanical 2-holed link

1 mint 22x25mm polymer clay "few words" pendant

1 brass 6x14mm hook clasp

1 gunmetal 4mm jump ring

2¾" of antiqued silver 4x5mm unsoldered etched cable chain

40" of green 1mm waxed cotton cord

TOOLS

Wire cutters

2 pairs of chain- or flat-nose pliers

Scissors

TECHNIQUE

Overhand knots, page 26

FINISHED SIZE

18½"

TIP

Save all your scraps from previous projects. You never know when you'll need an inch of chain or a single button.

1 Attach one end of 1⅜" of chain to one hole in the botanical link, opening and closing the chain links as you would jump rings. Attach the other end of the chain to the pendant. Repeat entire step with remaining chain.

2 String the left hole of the botanical link to the center of the cord. Use both cords to form an overhand knot. Snug knot against link. Use 1 cord to string 1E. Use the other cord to string 1E in the opposite direction. Form an overhand knot about ¼" from the previous knot.

3 Use 1 cord to string 1H. Use the other cord to string 1H in the opposite direction. Use both cords to form an overhand knot about ½" from the disc.

4 Repeat Step 3 eleven times, stringing beads in the following order: 1D, the ceramic heart (bottom to top), 1F, 1H, 1A, 1J, 1C, 1H, 1G, 1A, and 1 D. Trim cord ends.

5 Use the jump ring to attach the button and hook to the right hole of the link.

SHIMMERING PEARLS

ERIN SIEGEL

Sheer organza ribbon adds
subtle shimmer to the pearls
in this party-worthy
necklace.

MATERIALS

3 smoked topaz 6mm crystal bicones

13 gold 7x8mm potato pearls

12 copper 8x9mm potato pearls

5 bronze 14mm glass pearls

4 champagne 14mm glass pearls

4 ivory 14mm glass pearls

1 antique brass 35x11mm hook-and-eye clasp

1 antique brass 2½" head pin

8 antiqued brass 4.75mm jump rings

2 gold 2mm crimp tubes

50" of ivory 16mm organza ribbon

23" of bronze .019 beading wire

Fabric fray sealant

TOOLS

Wire cutters

Crimping pliers

2 pairs of chain- or flat-nose pliers

Round-nose pliers

Scissors

TECHNIQUES

Overhand knots, page 26

Square knots, page 26

Double-wrapped loops, page 23

FINISHED SIZE

18" (adjustable to 19")

TIP

If you don't have jump rings, use a short length of chain to create the necklace extension.

1   Use the head pin to string 1 crystal and 1 gold pearl; form a double-wrapped loop that attaches to 1 jump ring. *Use 1 jump ring to attach the previous jump ring to 1 jump ring. Repeat from * three times. Attach the last jump ring to the figure-eight half of the clasp.

2   Use the beading wire to string 1 crimp tube and the figure-eight half of the clasp; pass back through the tube and crimp. String 1 crystal. String {1 gold pearl and 1 copper pearl} six times.

3   Use the ribbon to form a loose overhand knot in the middle of the ribbon. String the knot on the beading wire and tighten just below the last pearl strung.

4   String 1 bronze pearl and form a square knot over the beading wire. Repeat twelve times, using 1 ivory pearl, 1 champagne pearl, 1 bronze pearl, 1 ivory pearl, 1 champagne pearl, 2 bronze pearls, 1 ivory pearl, 1 champagne pearl, 1 bronze pearl, 1 ivory pearl, and 1 champagne pearl. Dovetail ribbon ends by cutting from each corner to the middle. Trim ends to 1". Apply fabric fray sealant to ends. Let dry. Repeat Step 2, reversing the stringing sequence and using the hook half of the clasp.

PEARLY YOURS

LORELEI EURTO

Turn a striking button into a custom clasp for this romantic ribbon-and-chain necklace.

MATERIALS

1 lime green 10mm pressed-glass flower

1 green/brown/white 26x46mm pear pendant

1 brown-and-tan 25mm 2-holed Bakelite carved button

1 brass 2" head pin

18" of brass 6x9mm unsoldered etched cable chain

36" of olive ¾" silk ribbon

3" of copper 20-gauge wire

TOOLS

2 pairs of chain- or flat-nose pliers

Round-nose pliers

Wire cutters

TECHNIQUES

Overhand knot, page 26

Simple loops, page 23

Wrapped loops, page 23

FINISHED SIZE

19"

TIP

Frayed ribbon ends add to the romantic feel of this necklace.

1 Use the head pin to string the flower; form a wrapped loop that attaches to one end of the chain.

2 Use the silk ribbon to form an overhand knot on the previous chain link, leaving a ½" tail. Form a second overhand knot on top of the first.

3 Weave the ribbon loosely through the chain, alternating every other link. Repeat Step 2. Center the pendant on the ribbon. Open the middle chain link as you would a jump ring and attach the pendant.

4 Use the copper wire to form a simple loop. Bend the wire in half and thread each end through 1 buttonhole. Bend one wire into a long U-shape and form a simple loop at the end of the wire. Repeat with other wire. Flatten the wire against the back of the button. Attach the button clasp to the end of the chain without the flower dangle.

SWEET NECTAR

LORELEI EURTO

The movement of the hummingbird pendant and flower charm turn this necklace into a grown-up version of a childhood swing set.

MATERIALS

1 aqua-and-brown 48mm raku square tube

1 yellow 10mm Bakelite 2-holed flower button

1 silver-plated 12mm flower shank button

1 sterling silver 28mm hummingbird pendant

1 silver 3mm jump ring

20" of brown 1mm leather cord

6" of brass 24-gauge wire

3" of silver 20-gauge wire

TOOLS

Wire cutters

Round-nose pliers

2 pairs of chain- or flat-nose pliers

TECHNIQUES

Overhand knots, page 26

Wrapped-loop bail, page 24

Wire wrapping, page 25

FINISHED SIZE

17"

TIP

If you'd prefer that the pendant remain centered, add an overhand knot on either side.

1 Fold the cord in half. Use one end of the cord to string the tube. Use the other end to string the tube in the opposite direction. Center the tube on the cords, leaving about 2½" of loose cord below the tube. Form an overhand knot on the left side of the tube. Repeat for the right side.

2 Use the jump ring to attach the pendant to the cord below the tube. Use the silver wire to string one hole of the yellow button. Form a wrapped loop bail that attaches to the cord next to the pendant.

3 String the silver-plated button on one end of cord and fold over ¼". Use 3" of brass wire to wrap the cord ends. Fold about ½" of the other cord end. Use 3" of brass wire to wrap the cord ends, creating a ½" loop.

NOUVELLE

DENISE YEZBAK MOORE

Braiding sari silk and tucking it into large jump rings keep its easily frayed edges corralled, while still letting its luxurious texture and earthy tones shine.

MATERIALS

25 brown size 11° seed beads

2 cracked rainbow agate 8mm faceted rounds

24 cracked rainbow agate 12m faceted rounds

1 brass 18mm etched square ring

1 brass 7.5x67mm tall tag

2 brass 14x23mm flourish petal bead caps

2 brass 5mm jump rings

14 brass 15mm jump rings

2 brass 2mm crimp tubes

30" of cream 20mm sari silk

30" of aqua 20mm sari silk

30" of burnt umber 20mm sari silk

10" of brass 22-gauge wire

25" of .019 beading wire

TOOLS

Wire cutters

Round-nose pliers

2 pairs of chain- or flat-nose pliers

Crimping pliers

Scissors

Bail-making pliers (optional)

TECHNIQUES

Braiding, page 27

Overhand knots, page 26

Wrapped loops, page 23

FINISHED SIZE

18"

TIP

The uniform cylinders on bail-making pliers create the even loops for the handmade hook clasp. If you don't own bail-making pliers, use the largest part of your round-nose pliers.

1 Use bail-making or round-nose pliers to bend the end of the tall tag into a loop. About ¼" from the loop, bend the tag toward the loop. Leave a gap between this bend and the previous loop. About ½" from the previous bend, bend the tag in the opposite direction. Leave a gap between this bend and the previous bend. Set hook clasp aside.

2 Use the beading wire to string 1 crimp tube and one 15mm jump ring. Pass back through the crimp tube and crimp. String {1 seed bead and one 12mm cracked agate round} twenty-four times. String 1 seed bead, 1 crimp tube and one 15mm jump ring. Pass back through the crimp tube and crimp.

3 Use the 3 sari silk strands to form an overhand knot around the previous 15mm jump ring. Braid the strands for 14". Use all 3 strands to form an overhand knot around the other 15mm jump ring. Tighten strands. Trim.

4 Use one 15mm jump ring to attach the braided sari strand to the strung strand between the first and second agate round strung. Repeat eleven times, attaching the jump rings between every other agate round.

5 Use 5" of brass 22-gauge wire to form a wrapped loop. String one 8mm agate round and 1 bead cap. Form a wrapped loop that attaches to the previous 15mm jump ring at one end of the agate and silk strands. Gently close the petals of the bead cap around the knot. Use one 5mm jump ring to attach the hook clasp to the first wrapped loop in this step. Repeat entire step for the other side of the necklace, substituting the square ring for the hook clasp.

BLACK FLOWERS

TRACY STATLER

Adding space between the knots and beads allows the beads to slide around playfully on this goes-with-everything little black bracelet.

MATERIALS

1 white 6x18mm center-drilled stick pearl

2 crystal quartz 7–10mm chips

6 sterling silver 4mm large-holed rounds

3 silver 8x10mm flower barrels

2 sterling silver 3mm daisy spacers

1 sterling silver 16mm toggle clasp with two attached 4mm jump rings

2 sterling silver 22-gauge 1½" head pins

1 sterling silver 4mm jump ring

2 silver-plated 4x10mm fold-over cord ends

28½" of black 1.5mm leather cord

Instant adhesive

TOOLS

Scissors

Round-nose pliers

2 pairs of chain- or flat-nose pliers

Ruler

Bead stops

TECHNIQUES

Overhand knots, page 26

Wrapped loops, page 23

Fold-over cord ends, page 28

FINISHED SIZE

7"

TIP

If the bracelet keeps flipping upside down while worn, add dangles near the clasp. The additional weight will keep the toggle in place under your wrist.

1. Cut leather cord into 3 pieces. Center the 3 barrels on all 3 cords. Form an overhand knot on one side of the barrels, leaving a small gap for movement. Repeat on other side. Use 1 head pin to string 1 daisy spacer and the stick pearl; form a wrapped loop. Use 1 head pin to string 1 daisy spacer and the 2 crystal quartz chips; form a wrapped loop. Use the jump ring to attach the 2 dangles to the middle cord between 1 barrel and one center knot.

2. Use the top cord on the side with the dangles to form an overhand knot about ½" from the center knot. String 1 silver round and place a bead stop on the end of the cord. Use the middle cord to form an overhand knot about 1" from the center knot. String 1 silver round and place a bead stop on the end of the cord. Use the bottom cord to string 1 silver round and form an overhand knot about ½" from the center knot.

3. Use the top cord on the other side of the bracelet to form an overhand knot about 1½" from the center knot. Use the middle cord to form an overhand knot about ¼" form the center knot. String 1 silver round and place a bead stop on the end of the cord. Use the bottom cord to string 1 silver round and form an overhand knot about 1" from the center knot. String 1 silver round and place a bead stop on the end of the cord.

4. Remove the bead stops from the current side of the bracelet. Dab glue inside one cord end and place the ends of all 3 cords inside. Close and let dry. Use the 4mm jump ring attached to the bar half of the clasp to attach the cord end. Repeat entire step for other half of bracelet, using the ring half of the clasp.

GARDEN GRACES

LORELEI EURTO

Floral crepe silk cord, sometimes called kimono cord, adds an elegant touch to this romantic 2-strand bracelet.

MATERIALS

1 fuchsia 5mm crystal bicone

1 pink 5mm crystal bicone

6 blue 3x5mm faceted glass rondelles

6 purple 5mm faceted glass rounds

3 green 5mm faceted glass rounds

3 pink 5mm faceted glass rounds

2 cherry quartz 6x9mm faceted briolettes

2 olive jade 6x9mm faceted briolettes

1 orange jade 5x8mm faceted briolette

1 brass 6x3mm rondelle

24 brass 2mm cornerless cubes

1 green-and-melon 16mm ceramic heart charm

1 brass 25mm toggle ring

1 brass 5x30mm toggle bar

2 brass 2" head pins

4 brass 4mm jump rings

2 brass 7mm jump rings

1 brass 10mm jump ring

2 brass 10mm etched jump rings

2 brass 2mm crimp tubes

8" of black floral 5mm crepe silk cord

6" of brass 20-gauge wire

9" of .018 beading wire

TOOLS

Wire cutters

Round-nose pliers

2 pairs of chain- or flat-nose pliers

Crimping pliers

TECHNIQUES

Wire wrapping, page 25

Double-wrapped loops, page 23

FINISHED SIZE

8¼"

TIP

Use 2 jump rings between the crystals to create the illusion of a crystal dangle with a wire-wrapped middle.

1. String one 7mm jump ring on the cord. Leaving a ¾" tail, fold the cord end against the long cord. Use 3" of brass wire to wrap the cords together. Tuck in ends.

2. Use one 4mm jump ring to attach the previous 7mm jump ring to one 4mm jump ring. Use 1 head pin to string 1 cornerless cube and the toggle bar. Form a double-wrapped loop that attaches to the previous 4mm jump ring.

3. Use the beading wire to string 1 crimp tube and the previous 7mm jump ring; pass back through the crimp tube and crimp.

4. String 1 cornerless cube, 1 purple round, 1 cube, 1 blue rondelle, 1 cube, 1 green round, 1 cube, 1 cherry quartz briolette, 1 cube, 1 purple round, 1 cube, and 1 blue rondelle.* String 1 cube, 1 pink round, 1 cube, 1 olive jade briolette, 1 cube, 1 purple round, 1 cube, 1 blue rondelle, 1 cube, 1 pink round, 1 cube, and 1 orange jade briolette. Repeat through *. String 1 cube, 1 green round, 1 cube, 1 pink round, 1 cube, 1 olive jade briolette, 1 cube, 1 purple round, 1 cube, 1 blue rondelle, 1 crimp tube, and one 7mm jump ring. Pass back through the crimp tube and crimp. Use one 4mm jump ring to attach the previous 7mm jump ring to the toggle ring. Use 1 head pin to string 1 pink bicone, two 4mm jump rings, and 1 fuchsia bicone. Form a double-wrapped loop that attaches to the 10mm jump ring. Use one 4mm jump ring to attach the heart charm to the previous 10mm jump ring. Attach the 10mm jump ring to the toggle ring.

5. Repeat Step 1, attaching the other end of the cord to the 7mm jump ring used in Step 4. Use 1 etched jump ring to attach the beaded strand to the cord after the first olive jade briolette. Use 1 etched jump ring to attach the beaded strand to the cord after the second cherry quartz briolette.

BOHEMIAN WRAPSODY

TRACY STATLER

MATERIALS

6 brown 5mm rice pearls

6 champagne 6–7mm potato pearls

1 brown lip 16x24mm carved filigree shell rectangle

2 Thai silver 11mm flower shank buttons

12 sterling silver 21-gauge 1½" head pins

1 light latte 40" silk 18mm fairy ribbon

TOOLS

Round-nose pliers

Flat-nose pliers

TECHNIQUE

Wrapped loops, page 23

FINISHED SIZE

40"

Wear this carefree bracelet by wrapping the ribbon around your wrist several times and forming a knot. Change the bracelet's look by clustering the pearls tightly against the shell rectangle or scattering them several inches apart.

TIP

Make the wrapped loops on the pearl dangles the same size as the button shanks (about ⅛") to ensure that they stay on the ribbon.

1 Use 1 head pin to string 1 pearl; form a wrapped loop. Repeat eleven times for a total of 12 pearl dangles.

2 Center the shell rectangle on the silk ribbon, stringing from the bottom left hole to the bottom right hole, behind the back of the shell, and from the top right hole to the top left.

3 On the left ribbon, string 1 champagne pearl dangle, 1 flower button, 1 brown pearl dangle, 1 champagne pearl dangle, 2 brown pearl dangles, and 1 champagne pearl dangle. On the right ribbon, string 1 champagne pearl dangle, 1 flower button, 2 brown pearl dangles, 2 champagne pearl dangles, and 1 brown pearl dangle.

CROON

DENISE YEZBAK MOORE

MATERIALS

2 red 10mm ceramic rounds

10 brown/teal/white 16mm ceramic melon rounds

1 teal 40mm bird antique clay poker-chip pendant

1 brass 15mm jump ring

42" of black 1mm leather cord

TOOLS

Scissors

2 pairs of chain- or flat-nose pliers

TECHNIQUE

Overhand knots, page 26

FINISHED SIZE

7½"

Use a pendant to inspire a design as this designer did, pairing watermelon-like rounds and a sweet pair of bead-and-cord cherries with a whimsical bird pendant she created herself.

TIP

Spacing ceramic beads with knots reduces the chance of chipped beads.

1 To create the loop for the clasp, fold the leather in half. Use both cord ends to form an overhand knot about ¾" from the fold.

2 Sting 1 melon round; form an overhand knot. Attach the jump ring to the pendant and string the jump ring. String 1 melon round; form an overhand knot. Repeat seven times.

3 Use 1 cord to string 1 melon bead. Pass the cord through the melon bead a second time. Repeat entire step with other cord.

4 Wrap both cords below the melon bead; form an overhand knot.

5 String 1 red round onto one cord. Form an overhand knot about 1" from the previous overhand knot. Trim. Repeat entire step with other cord.

My Affection

LORELEI EURTO

Richly colored douppioni silk ribbon, woven with two colors, adds subtle shimmer to a bold, contemporary necklace.

MATERIALS

1 ivory-and-black 25mm porcelain disc

1 ivory-and-black 39mm ceramic square pendant

1 brass 7x14mm lobster clasp

5 brass 4mm jump rings

2 brass 9mm etched jump rings

1 brass 13x23mm rectangle jump ring

4 brass 9mm fold-over crimp ends

25" of brass 5x12mm unsoldered flat oval cable chain

24" of burgundy 13mm silk fairy ribbon

24" of purple 7mm silk douppioni ribbon

TOOLS

Scissors

2 pairs of chain- or flat-nose pliers

TECHNIQUE

Fold-over cord ends, page 28

FINISHED SIZE

25½"

TIP

For added security, dab glue inside the cord ends before closing.

1 Place one end of the burgundy ribbon inside one fold-over cord end and close. Repeat for other end of ribbon. Repeat entire step, using the purple ribbon. Set aside.

2 Use the rectangle jump ring to attach the disc bead and 1 etched jump ring to one end of the chain. *Use one 4mm jump ring to attach one end of the purple ribbon to the left of the chain. Use one 4mm jump ring to attach one end of the burgundy ribbon to the right of the chain.** Repeat from * to ** for the other ends of chain and ribbon. Use one 4mm jump ring to attach the clasp to the free end of chain.

3 Use the remaining etched jump ring to attach the pendant to both ribbons and link 16 of the chain from the lobster clasp.

AWAKENING LOTUS

MARY JANE DODD

A brass lotus link makes an ideal focal for this quietly empowering asymmetrical bracelet.

MATERIALS

2 sage 6mm lampwork rondelles

3 ivory 10mm lampwork rondelles

2 purple 12mm lampwork rondelles

1 sage 14mm lampwork rondelle

4 brass 2mm cornerless cubes

1 brass 39mm lotus link

4 brass 7mm jump rings

48" of olive drab 3-ply Irish waxed linen

72" of dark chocolate 3-ply Irish waxed linen

24" of dark brown 1.5mm leather cord

12" of antique brass 22-gauge wire

TOOLS

2 pairs of chain- or flat-nose pliers

Wire cutters

Scissors

Fabric glue

Ruler

Bracelet cone (optional)

2 clothespins or binder clips (optional)

TECHNIQUES

Lark's head knot, page 26

Overhand knot, page 26

Square knot, page 26

Wire wrapping, page 25

FINISHED SIZE

7"

TIP

A cone-shaped bracelet sizer measures a bracelet as it fits when worn. It's more accurate than a ruler when the bracelet contains large beads that reduce the bracelet's diameter.

1   Attach 1 jump ring to the left hole of the brass link. Repeat twice. Attach 1 jump ring to the previous 3 jump rings.

2   Use two 16" pieces of olive linen to form a lark's head knot on the previous jump ring.

3   Use all 4 linen strands to form an overhand knot. String 1 ivory rondelle and form an overhand knot. Use 2 strands to string 1 sage 6mm rondelle. Wrap the remaining 2 strands around the outside of the rondelle. Use all 4 strands to form an overhand knot.

4   String 1 purple rondelle and form an overhand knot.

5   Repeat Step 3. String 1 ivory rondelle and form an overhand knot twice, omitting the second sage rondelle. Repeat Step 4. Form a second overhand knot. String the sage 14mm rondelle and form an overhand knot. Tighten. Trim ends unevenly to ¼–½".

6   Center the second hole of the brass link on three 8" pieces of leather cord. Create the loop half of the clasp by folding the other ends of the cords about 3" from the link. Check that the loop fits snugly over the sage 14mm rondelle. If needed, secure cords with clothespins while measuring. Dab cords with fabric glue about 1" from the loop. Wrap the wire around the cords to secure. Tuck in the ends.

7   Leaving a 1½" tail, use the remaining olive linen to wrap the leather for about 1¼" starting about 1" from the link and working toward the loop. Repeat, moving in reverse from the loop to the link. Form a square knot, leaving a 1½" tail. Repeat entire step with remaining chocolate linen, taking care not to cover all the olive linen.

8   String 1 brass cornerless cube on one olive linen end. Form an overhand knot, about ¼" from the previous knot. Trim, leaving a ¹⁄₁₆" tail. Repeat three times for the remaining olive linen end and the two chocolate linen ends. Trim unevenly.

Ocean Love

LORELEI EURTO

Explore new color combinations by buying a mix of silk cords packaged together, such as the "Ocean Love" palette in this soothing necklace.

MATERIALS

10 aqua 12mm recycled glass rounds

1 pale yellow/mint/black 24mm ceramic textured round

11 brass 4mm melon rounds

1 brass 19x32mm swivel lobster clasp

2 brass 15mm jump rings

1 brass 2mm 4-prong cord end

48" of blue 4-ply waxed linen cord

9 assorted 42" silk 2mm cords in pale yellow, taupe, pale pink, turquoise, and light blue

TOOLS

Scissors

2 pairs of chain- or flat-nose pliers

TECHNIQUES

Braiding, page 27

Double overhand knot, page 26

Half-hitch knots, page 26

Overhand knot, page 26

FINISHED SIZE

22"

TIP

Securing silk cords with half-hitch knots is a clever alternative to using wirewrapping or crimp ends.

1   Center all 9 strands of silk cord on 1 jump ring.

2   Use 16" of linen cord to form a half-hitch knot around the silk cords close to the jump ring. Repeat eight times, wrapping the linen cord around the silk cords and covering the linen cord's tail. Form two half-hitch knots and a double overhand knot. Trim.

3   Group the silk cords into three 6-cord sections. Braid the three groups of cords for about 12". Use 1 jump ring to string the cord ends and fold them against the braid. Repeat Step 2, creating sixteen half-hitch knots instead of eleven.

4   Center the lobster clasp on 16" of linen cord and form an overhand knot. Use both cords to string {1 glass round and 1 brass round} seven times. String the ceramic round. String {1 brass round and 1 glass round} three times. String 1 brass round; form an overhand knot. Insert the knot into the cord end. Use chain- or flat-nose pliers to close prongs tightly around knot. Use 1 jump ring attached to one end of the the braid to attach the cord end.

SONORAN SUNSET

TRACY STATLER

Nature often provides
the best color palettes,
as demonstrated by the
vibrant pinks, oranges,
and yellows in this sunset-
inspired necklace.

MATERIALS

1 fuchsia 10x6mm faceted pressed-glass rondelle

11 assorted 8mm agate rounds

3 copper 28x41mm hammered teardrop rings

7 copper 22-gauge 2" head pins

7 copper 6mm jump rings

20" of chocolate brown 10mm deerskin leather lace

TOOLS

Scissors

2 pairs of chain- or flat-nose pliers

Leather punch

Ruler

TECHNIQUES

Wrapped loops, page 23

Leather hole punching, page 28

FINISHED SIZE

24"

TIP

Eliminating the clasp from a long necklace design makes it more affordable.

1   Use 1 head pin to string 2 agate rounds; form a wrapped loop. Repeat four times for a total of 5 double agate dangles. Use 1 head pin to string 1 agate round; form a wrapped loop. Use 1 head pin to string the glass rondelle; form a wrapped loop. Set aside.

2   Punch a 1.5mm hole in the center of one end of leather lace, about ⅛" from the end. Use 1 jump ring to attach the hole in the leather lace to 1 jump ring. Attach the previous jump ring to 1 teardrop ring.

3   Use 1 jump ring to attach the previous teardrop ring to 2 double dangles and 1 teardrop ring.

4   Repeat Step 2 for other end of leather lace. Use 1 jump ring to attach 1 double dangle and the single agate round dangle to the previous teardrop ring. Use 1 jump ring to attach 2 double dangles, the glass rondelle dangle, and the 2 teardrop rings connected to the cord ends.

IN THE GARDEN

ERIN SIEGEL

Use a slipknot to transform this glass and ceramic necklace from princess to matinee length.

MATERIALS

7 orange-and-green 8x6mm pressed-glass rondelles

5 light blue Picasso 10mm pressed-glass coins

4 green Picasso 10mm pressed-glass coins

3 green 8x18mm pressed-glass marquis

3 blue-and-orange 14mm glass teardrops

1 terra-cotta 27x66mm floral ceramic pendant

2 sterling silver 6mm soldered jump rings

2 sterling silver 3mm knot cups

42" of burnt orange 15mm fairy silk ribbon

79" (1 card) of jade green size 8 silk beading cord with attached needle

Fabric cement

TOOLS

Scissors

Knotting tweezers

Crimping pliers

TECHNIQUES

Knotting with tweezers, page 27

Overhand knots, page 26

Lark's head knots, page 26

Knot cups, page 28

Slipknots, page 27

Double overhand knots, page 26

FINISHED SIZE

18½" (adjustable to 26")

TIP

If you'd prefer to use a slide knot (page 27), substitute a cord for the ribbon. Not only would the stiffer cord hold the knot better, but it would be easier to see its decorative wraps.

1 Remove the silk cord from the card. Stretch a small section at a time. Form a double overhand knot at the end opposite the needle. Dab knot with glue; let dry. Trim tail. String 1 knot cup, close and attach to 1 jump ring. Form an overhand knot. Snug against the knot cup.

2 String the beads in the following order, forming an overhand knot after each bead: 1 teardrop, 1 rondelle, 1 green coin, 2 blue coins, 1 teardrop, 1 marquis, 1 rondelle, 1 green coin, 1 blue coin, and 1 rondelle. Form three overhand knots.

3 Use a lark's head knot to attach the pendant snug against the previous knot. Form three overhand knots. String the beads in the following order, forming an overhand knot after each bead: 1 marquis, 1 green coin, 1 teardrop, 2 rondelles, 1 blue coin, 1 marquis, 1 rondelle, 1 green coin, 1 blue coin, and 1 rondelle. String 1 knot cup. Form a double overhand knot inside the knot cup. Dab knot with glue; let dry. Close knot cup and trim cord. Attach the knot cup to 1 jump ring.

4 Center 1 jump ring on the ribbon. Use the opposite jump ring to string both ribbon ends. Use both ends of the ribbon to form a slipknot just above the first jump ring, leaving a 3½" tail.

BUTTERFLY SONG

ERIN SIEGEL

Tie the soft leather lace
in a bow to wear this
Southwest-inspired
necklace.

MATERIALS

1 g of silver size 11° seed beads

24 turquoise jasper 6mm rice

12 amazonite 6mm rounds

26 wood 6mm bicones

4 green-and-blue 10mm ceramic rounds

1 turquoise 38mm ceramic butterfly pendant

6 sterling silver 2" head pins

5 sterling silver 8mm closed jump rings

6 sterling silver 2mm crimp tubes

6 sterling silver 3mm crimp covers

2 antiqued pewter 12x6.5mm crimp cord ends

31" of light brown 5mm deerskin leather lace

8" of sterling silver 24-gauge wire

6" of sterling silver 20-gauge wire

36" of .019 beading wire

TOOLS

Chain-nose pliers

Round-nose pliers

Wire cutters

Crimping pliers

TECHNIQUES

Crimp cord ends, page 28

Crimp covers, page 22

Wrapped-loop bail, page 24

Wire wrapping, page 25

Wrapped loops, page 23

FINISHED SIZE

18" (adjustable)

TIP: *Multiple jump rings make a secure and affordable bail for a wire-wrapped pendant.*

1 Fold ¼" of one end of 15½" of leather lace and insert into one cord end. Flatten. Repeat for other leather lace.

2 Use 12" of beading wire to string 1 crimp tube and the ring on one cord end; pass back through the tube and crimp. Cover the crimp tube with 1 crimp cover.

3 String {1 seed bead and 1 turquoise jasper} eleven times.

4 String 3 seed beads and 3 jump rings. Repeat Step 3, reversing the stringing sequence.

5 String 1 crimp tube and the ring on the other cord end; pass back through the tube. Crimp and cover.

6 Repeat Step 2.

7 String 3 wood bicones, 1 ceramic round, 6 wood bicones, 1 ceramic round, and 3 wood bicones.

8 String 3 seed beads and the 3 previous jump rings. Repeat Step 7, reversing the stringing sequence. Repeat Step 5.

9 Repeat Step 2. String 3 seed beads.

10 String {1 amazonite round and 8 seed beads} four times.

11 String the 3 jump rings from Step 4. Repeat Step 10. String 1 amazonite and 3 seed beads. Repeat Step 5.

12 Use the 20-gauge wire to form a wrapped-loop bail that attaches the ceramic pendant to the previous 3 jump rings.

13 Use 1 head pin to string 1 turquoise jasper and form a wrapped loop that attaches to 1 jump ring. Repeat using 1 amazonite round. Repeat using 1 wood bicone. Repeat entire step using the remaining jump ring. Set the beaded jump rings aside.

14 Use the free end of 1 leather lace to string 1 beaded jump ring. Fold ½" of lace over the beaded jump ring. Use 4" of 24-gauge wire to wrap around the folded leather five times. Repeat entire step for other side of the necklace.

Afternoon Tea

ERIN SIEGEL

The combination of elegant silk ribbon and denim-blue gemstones and crystals creates a lariat necklace that works equally well with a crisp linen dress or jeans.

MATERIALS

17 Montana blue 4mm crystal bicones

18 white 5mm top-drilled heishi pearls

2 white 6mm potato pearls

17 sodalite 4mm rounds

2 blue 14mm delicate scrolls ceramic rounds

4 copper 7mm star spacers

6 antique copper 2.5" ball-end head pins

2 antique copper 6mm jump rings

1 copper 40" handpainted ¹³⁄₁₆" silk ribbon

24" of antique copper 24-gauge wire

12" of antique cooper 20-gauge wire

TOOLS

Wire cutters

Round-nose pliers

2 pairs of chain- or flat-nose pliers

Ruler

TECHNIQUES

Simple loops, page 23

Double-wrapped loops, page 23

Wire wrapping, page 25

FINISHED SIZE

38"

TIP

The beaded wire wrapping at the front of the lariat is not merely decorative; the added weight keeps the lariat in place when worn.

1 Use 1 head pin to string 1 potato pearl; form a double-wrapped loop. Repeat using 1 crystal bicone. Repeat using 1 sodalite round. Repeat entire step. Set dangles aside.

2 Use 6" of 20-gauge wire to form a simple loop that attaches to 1 crystal bicone dangle, 1 potato pearl dangle, and 1 sodalite dangle. String 1 copper spacer, 1 ceramic round, and 1 copper spacer; form a double-wrapped loop. Repeat entire step. Set aside ceramic dangles.

3 String 1 jump ring onto one end of the ribbon. Fold the ribbon back onto itself about 1" from the end. *Use 8" of 24-gauge wire to wrap around the folded ribbon five times. String {1 heishi pearl, 1 crystal, and 1 sodalite} five times. String 1 heishi pearl and wrap around the ribbon five times.** Use the previous jump ring to attach 1 ceramic dangle. Repeat entire step for the other end of the ribbon.

4 Fold the ribbon so that one end is about 1½" longer than the other. About 1¾" from the fold, repeat Step 3 from * to **.

WITCH HAZEL

LORELEI EURTO

MATERIALS

32 matte metallic luster rainbow gold green size 6° seed beads

16 assorted 3–6x11–22mm top-drilled sticks in tigereye, unakite, and orange jade

1 coconut 40mm filigree 4-holed button

1 tin 28mm "Witch Hazel" round box link

15" of green size 16 silk cord

Fabric cement

TOOLS

Scissors

TECHNIQUES

Overhand knots, page 26

Square knots, page 26

FINISHED SIZE

7½"

Silk cord, frayed with the use of flat-nose pliers, adds a whimsical touch to this gemstone bracelet.

TIP

Buttons make unique and affordable clasps.

1 Use the silk cord to string two center buttonholes, leaving a 1½" tail. Use both cords to form an overhand knot. Snug the knot against the button.

2 String 1 stick bead; form an overhand knot. Repeat twelve times. String the tin box link and form an overhand knot.

3 String 1 stick bead and form an overhand knot. Repeat twice. String all 32 seed beads and form a square knot just below the previous knot. Dab knot with glue. Let dry. Fray the ends of the cord.

SOUL SISTER

ERIN SIEGEL

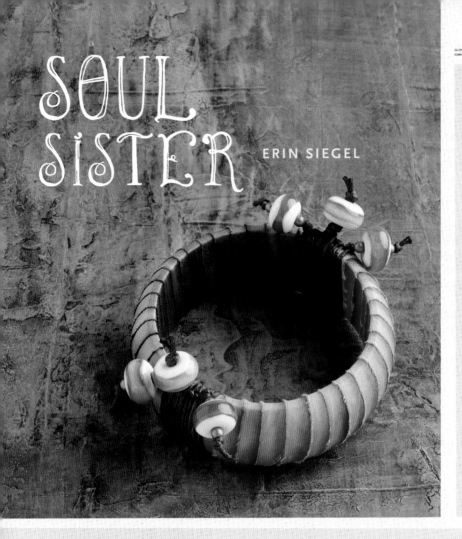

MATERIALS

6 assorted 8x12mm lampwork rondelles in ivory/brown/purple

8 antique copper 3.5mm rounds

1 wood 2⅝" (interior diameter) lacquered bangle

36" of brown 1mm cotton cord

45" of cymbidium ⁷⁄₁₆" hand-dyed silk ribbon

45" of abalone ⁷⁄₁₆" hand-dyed silk ribbon

Fabric glue

TOOLS

Scissors

TECHNIQUES

Square knots, page 26

Half-hitch knots, page 26

Double overhand knots, page 26

Lark's head knots, page 26

Overhand knots, page 26

FINISHED SIZE

7½"

Colorful hand-dyed silk ribbon turns a plain wood bangle into a stylish accessory.

TIP
Bangle bracelets make great gifts since they easily fit a range of wrist sizes.

1   Dab glue on one end of the cymbidium ribbon and adhere inside bangle. Let dry. Wrap the ribbon around half of the bangle, slightly overlapping the wraps. Dab glue on the other end of the ribbon and adhere to the ribbon on the inside of the bangle. Repeat entire step using the abalone ribbon and the other half of the bangle.

2   Leaving a 3" tail, use 12" of cotton cord to form a square knot ¼" from the seam of the 2 ribbons. Use the longer cord to form nine half-hitch knots across the top of the bangle, covering the ribbon seam. Form a double overhand knot. *Use 1 cord to string 1 copper round, 1 lampwork rondelle, and 1 copper round; form a double overhand knot.** Repeat from * to ** using the other cord. Use 6" of cord to form a lark's head knot at the center of the half-hitch knots. Use both cords to form an overhand knot. Use both cords to string 1 rondelle and form an overhand knot.

3   Repeat Step 2 for the other half of the bracelet.

eCLeCTiC eRiN

DENISE YEZBAK MOORE

Create this striking necklace in under an hour using inexpensive craft store materials, including a typewriter key clasp that moonlights as a decorative dangle.

MATERIALS

4 ivory 8x6mm wood rondelles

1 black 8x6mm wood rondelle

4 black-and-brown 15mm wood rounds

2 black-and-brown 23x18mm wood barrels

2 black-and-brown 18x25mm wood teardrops

2 black 15x30–34mm ceramic rectangles

1 silver 25mm leaf coin

1 silver 17x25mm leaf oval

1 silver/ivory/black 14x62mm domino link

1 silver-and-black 18x34mm typewriter-key hook clasp

40" of black 2mm leather cord

TOOLS

Scissors

Ruler

TECHNIQUES

Overhand knots, page 26

FINISHED SIZE

20"

TIP

When creating a necklace with large beads, use hollow or light-weight beads to ensure that the necklace is not too heavy to be worn comfortably.

1 String the typewriter key half of the clasp and form an overhand knot about 1½" from the cord end. Form an overhand knot about ¾" from the previous knot. String the hook half of the clasp. Form an overhand knot. String 1 ivory rondelle; form an overhand knot.

2 String the remaining beads in this order, forming an overhand knot between each one: 1 black rondelle, 1 ivory rondelle, the domino link, 1 ivory rondelle, 1 wood round, the silver oval, 1 wood round, 1 teardrop (wide end first), 1 black rectangle, 1 wood round, 1 barrel, the silver coin, 1 barrel, 1 rectangle, 1 teardrop (narrow end first), 1 ivory rondelle, and 1 wood round.

3 Fold the remaining cord in half. Leaving a 1½" tail, use both cords to form an overhand knot about 1½" from the fold. Use both cords to form a second overhand knot below the first.

FLiRTaTiON LaRiaT

LORELEI EURTO

Traditionally used for
chokers, velvet ribbon
makes a luxurious lariat.

MATERIALS

28 assorted 4mm crystal bicones in rose, golden shadow, crystal, black diamond

13 assorted 6mm crystal bicones in rose, golden shadow, crystal, black diamond

13 champagne 10mm glass pearls

39 brass 1½" 24-gauge head pins

15 brass 7mm jump rings

2 brass 1" ribbon crimp ends

4" of brass 16mm/12mm unsoldered round cable chain

47" of purple 1" hand-dyed velvet ribbon

TOOLS

2 pairs of chain- or flat-nose pliers

Round-nose pliers

Wire cutters

TECHNIQUES

Ribbon ends, page 28

Wrapped loops, page 23

FINISHED SIZE

53"

TIP

Thin (24–26-gauge) head pins are sometimes called pearl head pins since they fit small bead holes.

1 Use 1 head pin to string 1 pearl; form a wrapped loop. Repeat twelve times. Use 1 head pin to string one 6mm bicone; form a wrapped loop. Repeat ten times. Use 1 head pin to string two 4mm bicones; form a wrapped loop. Repeat twelve times. Use 1 head pin to string one 6mm bicone and one 4mm bicone; form a wrapped loop. Repeat. Mix the 26 crystal dangles together and set aside.

2 Attach one ribbon end to one end of the velvet ribbon. Use 1 jump ring to attach the ribbon end to the large (16mm) link of 2" (4 links) of chain. Separate the chain links as you would jump rings. Use 1 jump ring to attach 1 pearl dangle and 2 crystal dangles to the previous large chain link. Repeat, attaching the jump ring to the other side of the link. Use 1 jump ring to attach 1 pearl dangle and 2 crystal dangles to the second chain link. Repeat entire step for the last 2 chain links.

3 Repeat Step 2 for the other half of necklace, adding an extra jump ring with 1 pearl dangle and 2 crystal dangles on the second chain link.

iNDiGO FOREST

ERIN SIEGEL

Knotted teal linen adds texture
and color to this peaceful wood,
silver, and ceramic necklace.

MATERIALS

24 wood 6mm rounds

12 wood 10x13mm triangles

2 indigo 12mm ceramic rounds

20 sterling silver 2mm rounds

1 indigo 44x51mm ceramic oval pendant

1 sterling silver 25x13mm hammered spiral hook-and-eye clasp

96" of teal 4-ply Irish waxed linen cord

TOOLS

Scissors

Ruler

TECHNIQUES

Overhand knots, page 26

Slipknots, page 27

FINISHED SIZE

18"

TIP

Because this slipknot is attached to a clasp, it won't move as a normal slipknot would.

1. Cut cord in four 24" pieces. Use all 4 cords to form an overhand knot about 3" from the ends. Use 2 cords to string the pendant (front to back), keeping the knot and tails hanging in front. Use 1 tail to string 1 wood round and 1 silver round; form an overhand knot. Repeat three times for the remaining 3 tails, staggering the tail lengths. Trim ends.

2. Use the 2 cords on the left side of the pendant to form an overhand knot. *Use 1 cord to string 1 wood triangle. Use both cords to form an overhand knot.** Repeat from * to ** twice. Use both cords to string 1 ceramic round; form an overhand knot. Repeat from * to ** six times.

3. Use 1 cord to string 1 wood round. Use both cords to form an overhand knot. Repeat entire step six times.

4. Use both cords to string the hook half of the clasp and form a slipknot. Use 1 cord to string 1 silver round. Form an overhand knot ¼" from the previous knot. Trim. Use the other cord to string 1 silver round. Form an overhand knot ½" from the previous slipknot. Trim.

5. Use the 2 cords on the right side of the pendant to form an overhand knot. *Use 1 cord to string 1 silver round, 1 wood round, and 1 silver round. Form an overhand knot. Form an overhand knot about ½" from the previous knot.** Repeat from * to ** twice.

6. Use the other cord to form an overhand knot about ½" from the previous knot. String 1 silver round, 1 wood round, and 1 silver round. Form an overhand knot. Repeat entire step twice.

7. Use both cords to form an overhand knot. Use both cords to string 1 ceramic round and form an overhand knot. Repeat Step 2 from * to ** three times. Repeat Step 3. Repeat Step 4, using the ring half of the clasp.

POMPIDOU

LORELEI EURTO

With a total cost under $20, this cheerful necklace proves you don't have to spend a fortune to make boutique-style jewelry.

MATERIALS

28 red size 6° seed beads

1 red 60mm seed bead pom-pom link with two attached brass 7mm jump rings

5 wood 6x10mm ovals

5 wood 16x8mm carved wheels

2 gunmetal 6mm jump rings

2 gunmetal 3mm fold-over crimp ends

1 silver 3mm crimp tube

12" of brown 4-ply waxed linen cord

32" of red 5mm satin ribbon

Instant adhesive

TOOLS

Scissors

2 pairs of chain- or flat-nose pliers

Crimping pliers

TECHNIQUES

Overhand knots, page 26

Fold-over cord ends, page 28

FINISHED SIZE

18" (adjustable)

TIP

Use crimping pliers on linen cord just as you would with beading wire.

1 Center 1 jump ring on the linen cord. Use both cord ends to form an overhand knot just below the jump ring.

2 Use both cords to string 1 wood wheel. Use 1 cord to string 1 wood oval, the first jump ring on the pom-pom link, 3 wood ovals, the second jump ring on the link, and 1 wood oval. Use the other cord to string both links on the pom-pom link.

3 Use both cords to string 1 wood wheel; form an overhand knot. Use 1 cord to string 2 seed beads. Use the other cord to string 2 seed beads. Use both cords to form an overhand knot. Repeat entire step six times.

4 Use both cords to string 1 wood wheel and form an overhand knot. Use both cords to string the crimp tube and 1 jump ring. Pass the cords back through the crimp tube and crimp.

5 Insert 16" of ribbon into one fold-over cord end. Dab with glue and close. Let dry. Attach the previous jump ring to the cord end. Repeat entire step for other half of necklace.

LEATHER RUFFLE HOOPS

ERIN SIEGEL

MATERIALS

20 coral 4mm crystal pearls

2 sterling silver 35mm hammered 18-gauge hoops

16¼" of tan ³⁄₁₆" deerskin leather lace

48" of copper 24-gauge wire

TOOLS

Wire cutters

Chain-nose pliers

¹⁄₁₆" leather hole punch

Scissors

Ruler

Pen

TECHNIQUES

Leather hole punching, page 28

Wire wrapping, page 25

FINISHED SIZE

1¾"

Leather lace adds a burst of texture to these stylish hoops.

TIP

If your wire wraps are too loose, slide the wire firmly against the leather and crimp the wire onto the hoop with chain-nose pliers.

1 Cut the leather lace in half. Lay 1 leather strip on the ruler. Use the pen to mark the center of the leather ⅛" from the end. Mark the remaining leather every ½". Punch holes through all the marked places in the leather.

2 Use 12" of wire to tightly wrap 1 silver hoop three times, beginning at the hoop's loop. *Bring the wire to the top of the hoop and string 1 coral pearl. Hold the pearl at the top of the hoop and wrap the wire three times around the hoop.** Repeat from * to ** four times.

3 String the leather onto the hoop, passing the end of the hoop through each hole. Gather the leather up to the last wire-wrapped bead. Twist the leather with your fingers and scrunch it against the last bead. While holding the leather, use 12" of wire to wrap three times around the hoop against the twisted leather. *String 1 pearl onto the wire and wrap three times.** Repeat from * to ** four times.

4 Repeat Steps 1–3 to make the second earring.

FLEUR-DE-LIS

ERIN SIEGEL

MATERIALS

9 turquoise 13mm corrugated wood rounds

1 black-and-white 25mm fleur-de-lis 2-hole plastic button

48" of black 2mm twisted cotton cord

TOOLS

Scissors

TECHNIQUE

Overhand knots, page 26

FINISHED SIZE

8"

You only need a pair of scissors and one knotting technique to make this modern bracelet.

TIP

If you use a button with a shank on the back, skip Step 3. Instead, use both cords to form an overhand knot around the shank and trim.

1 Fold the cotton cord in half. Use both cords to form an overhand knot about 1¼" from the fold.

2 Use 1 cord to string 1 turquoise round. Use both cords to form an overhand knot after the round. Repeat entire step eight times.

3 Use 1 cord to string 1 buttonhole. Use the other cord to string the other buttonhole. Use both cords to form an overhand knot. Trim ends to ¼" and fray.

QUeeN aNNe's Lace

LORELEI EURTO

Give antique lace an updated look by weaving it with leather cording.

MATERIALS

1 brown 40mm ceramic floral pendant

1 steel 10x21mm hook clasp

1 gunmetal 4mm jump ring

2 gunmetal 5mm jump rings

9" of antiqued silver 6x7mm/7x9mm/10x11mm flat cable chain

18" of white 18mm vintage lace

20" of brown 1.5mm leather cord

10" of violet 2mm silk cord

3" of green 1mm size 16 silk cord

TOOLS

2 pairs of chain- or flat-nose pliers

Scissors

TECHNIQUE

Square knot, page 26

FINISHED SIZE

22³⁄₄"

TIP

Instead of cutting apart chain and wasting links, simply fold it for a mulistrand look.

1 Weave leather cord through the bottom holes of the lace, leaving a 1½" tail at each end.

2 Use 1 tail to string one 5mm jump ring. Use 5" of violet silk cord to wrap the leather tail and lace just below the jump ring. Form a square knot. Trim leather tail and silk to ¼". Repeat entire step for the other half of necklace.

3 Fold the chain in half. Attach both ends to the previous jump ring. Use the 4mm jump ring to attach the clasp to the middle chain link.

4 Center the pendant and the middle link of one chain on the green silk cord. Form a square knot. Trim ends to ¼" and fray.

SIMPLY PEACEFUL

ERIN SIEGEL

Use a touch of leather cord to high-
light a handmade ceramic pendant in
this simple asymmetrical necklace.

MATERIALS

56 carnelian 6mm rounds

1 peach 27x36mm ceramic Chinese "peace" teardrop pendant

8 copper 2mm rounds

1 copper 27mm hammered S-clasp with two attached 7mm jump rings

1 copper 3" head pin

2 copper 2mm crimp tubes

2 copper 4mm crimp covers

16" of natural 2mm leather cord

18" of copper .019 beading wire

TOOLS

Wire cutters

Crimping pliers

Chain-nose pliers

Round-nose pliers

Scissors

TECHNIQUES

Crimp covers, page 22

Double-wrapped loops, page 23

Lark's head knots, page 26

Overhand knots, page 26

FINISHED SIZE

18"

TIP

Instead of hiding a beautiful clasp at the back of the necklace, show it off in the front.

1   Use the head pin to string 1 carnelian round and form a double-wrapped loop. Set aside.

2   Use the cord to form a lark's head knot on the pendant. *Fold 3" of one end of the cord back onto itself. Use both ends to form an overhand knot, leaving a ½" loop.** Use the free end of the cord to string the carnelian dangle from Step 1. Repeat from * to ** with the other end of the cord.

3   Use the beading wire to string 1 crimp tube, 8 copper rounds, and the first leather loop created in Step 2. Pass back through the tube and crimp. Cover the crimp tube with 1 crimp cover. String 55 carnelian rounds, 1 crimp tube, and one of the jump rings on the clasp; pass back through the tube. Crimp and cover. Use the other jump ring on the clasp to attach the remaining leather loop.

CAREY

DENISE YEZBAK MOORE

Silk ribbon adds a romantic touch to this beaded chain necklace, which features a handcrafted bail made with brass filigree.

MATERIALS

16 amazonite 5x7mm faceted rondelles

16 laborite 8x9mm faceted rondelles

1 turquoise-and-chocolate 30x38 ceramic teardrop pendant

2 brass 3mm rounds

1 brass 22mm hammered ring

1 brass 7x29mm etched creative bar

1 brass 22x64mm diamond trellis filigree

3 brass 3" head pins

16 brass 7mm jump rings

4 brass 9mm etched jump rings

12 brass 10mm jump rings

56" of brass 24-gauge wire

16½" of brass 3.5x4mm unsoldered flat cable chain

24" of brown ½" silk ribbon

TOOLS

Wire cutters

Round-nose pliers

2 pairs of chain- or flat-nose pliers

Bail-making pliers (optional)

Metal file (optional)

TECHNIQUES

Wrapped loops, page 23

Overhand knots, page 26

FINISHED SIZE

17"

1   Bend the center of the filigree trellis back and forth until it breaks into two pieces. Put one piece of the trellis away for future use. If necessary, file any sharp edges on the remaining piece. Use bail-making pliers or round-nose pliers to bend ¼" of the pointed tip of the trellis until it touches itself. Bend the center of the trellis in half, away from the tip. Use 1 etched jump ring to attach the left corner of the filigree to 1 etched jump ring. Use 1 etched jump ring to attach the right corner of the filigree to the previous etched jump ring. Use the remaining etched jump ring to attach the pendant to the previous etched jump ring. Set filigree bail aside.

2   Use 2" of brass wire to form a wrapped loop. String 1 laborite rondelle and form a wrapped loop. Use 2" of brass wire to form a wrapped loop that connects to the previous wrapped loop. String 1 amazonite rondelle and form wrapped loop. Repeat entire step six times.

3   Use 1 head pin to string 1 brass round, 1 amazonite rondelle, and 1 laborite rondelle. Form a wrapped loop that attaches to the previous wrapped loop.

4   Repeat Steps 2–3 for other half of necklace. Use one 7mm jump ring to attach the hammered brass ring to one end of the chain and the first wrapped loop of the beaded chain. Center the filigree bail on the chain. Use 1 head pin to string 1 amazonite and the creative bar (etched side up). Form a wrapped loop. Use one 7mm jump ring to attach the bar to the other end of chain and the first wrapped loop of the second beaded chain.

5   Use the silk ribbon to form an overhand knot around the 7mm jump ring below the hammered ring, leaving a ½" tail. Form a second knot above the first. Use the ribbon to string the filigree bail. Form an overhand knot around the 7mm jump ring below the creative bar, leaving a ½" tail. Form a second knot above the first. Trim.

6   Use one 10mm jump ring to secure the chain, ribbon, and beaded links about ½" from the previous jump ring. Use one 7mm jump ring to secure the chain, ribbon, and beaded links about ½" from the previous jump ring. Repeat entire step six times.

7   Repeat Step 6 for other half of necklace.

batik boutique

LORELEI EURTO

This beach-worthy necklace cleverly hides a hook clasp behind a knotted ribbon, giving the illusion that the necklace is tied closed.

MATERIALS

3 wood 25x53mm marquis rings

1 blue-and-green 45mm ceramic 4-holed button

1 brass 6x14mm hook clasp

6 brass 2" head pins

1 brass 7mm jump ring

1 brass 15mm jump ring

6" of brown 3-ply twisted 1mm nylon cord

36" of blue-and-yellow 18mm floral cotton ribbon

3½" of brass 22-gauge wire

3½" of brass 20-gauge wire

TOOLS

Wire cutters

Round-nose pliers

2 pairs of chain- or flat-nose pliers

Scissors

TECHNIQUES

Wrapped loop, page 23

Wrapped-loop bail, page 24

Square knot, page 26

Wire wrapping, page 25

FINISHED SIZE

23½"

TIP

Use a wrapped loop instead of a jump ring to turn a large button into a link.

1 Use the 20-gauge wire to string 1 buttonhole; form a wrapped-loop bail. Set aside.

2 Use 1 head pin to string the hole (inside to outside) of 1 wood ring. Form a wrapped loop that attaches to the 15mm jump ring. *Use 1 head pin to string the other hole (inside to outside) of the ring; form a wrapped loop. Use 1 head pin to string the hole (inside to outside) of 1 wood ring. Form a wrapped loop that attaches to the previous wrapped loop.** Repeat from * to ** twice, attaching the last wrapped loop to the wrapped-loop bail on the button.

3 Center the buttonhole opposite the bail on the ribbon. Wrap the cord four times around the ribbon, snug against the button. Form a square knot and trim cord ends to ¼".

4 Use both ribbons to string the 7mm jump ring, leaving 3" tails. Wrap the 22-gauge wire around the ribbon, snug against the jump ring. Use both ribbons to form an overhand knot. Attach the clasp to the previous jump ring.

COPPER ANTIQUITY

ERIN SIEGEL

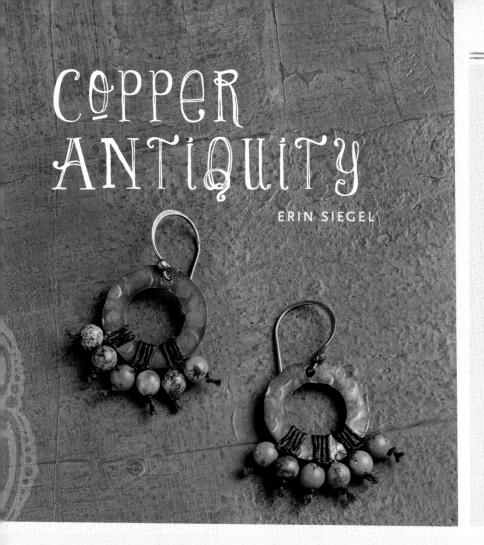

MATERIALS

12 turquoise 5mm rounds

2 copper 20mm hammered washers

2 antique copper hammered ear wires

56" of chocolate brown 4-ply Irish waxed linen cord

TOOLS

Scissors

Ruler

Chain-nose pliers

TECHNIQUES

Lark's head knots, page 26

Overhand knots, page 26

Half-hitch knots, page 26

FINISHED SIZE

1¾"

The striking combination of antiqued copper findings, turquoise, and linen cord make these earrings look like relics from ancient times.

TIP

To ensure that the earrings are perfectly balanced, the beads are first wrapped directly across from the hole and then on either side, rather than working from left to right.

1   Fold 3" of the 28" cord. Use both cords to form a lark's head knot on the washer, opposite the hole.

2   Use the short cord to string 1 turquoise round and form an overhand knot. Trim end to ⅛". Use the long cord to form two half-hitch knots around the copper washer. String 1 turquoise round; form an overhand knot. Trim end to ⅛".

3   Repeat Step 2 on the left side of the center pair of turquoise rounds. Repeat Step on the right side of the center rounds. Attach 1 ear wire to the washer's hole.

4   Repeat Steps 1–3 for second earring.

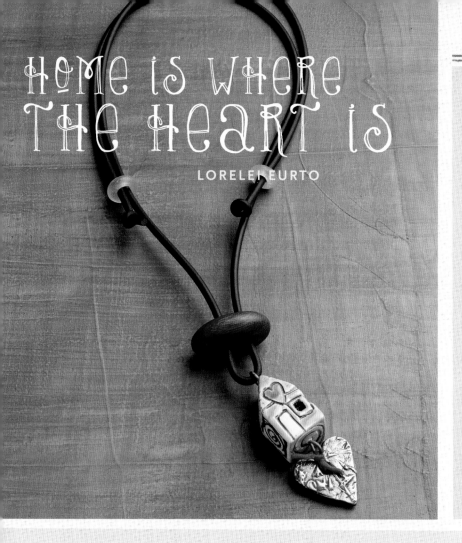

HOME IS WHERE THE HEART IS

LORELEI EURTO

MATERIALS

2 clear 12mm frosted glass rings

1 wood 15x30mm 2-holed button

1 multicolored 17x45mm ceramic house link

1 pewter 25x28mm heart pendant

3" of red 2mm silk cord

30" of black 3mm rubber cord

TOOLS

Scissors

TECHNIQUES

Square knot, page 26

Overhand knot, page 26

FINISHED SIZE

16" (adjustable to 20")

Use glass rings and simple knots to adjust the length of this whimsical necklace.

TIP

Instead of using glass rings, create a sliding knot (page 27) with cord.

1 Center the top loop of the house link on rubber cord. Use 1 cord to string 1 buttonhole. Use the other cord to string the other buttonhole. Snug the button against the house link. Use 1 cord to string 1 ring. Use the other cord to string the remaining ring.

2 Use the left cord to string the ring on the right side (top to bottom). Form an overhand knot at the end of the cord. Trim to ¼". Use the right cord to string the ring on the left side (top to bottom). Form an overhand knot at the end of the cord. Trim to ¼".

3 Use the silk cord to string the heart pendant from the bottom loop of the house link. Form a square knot. Trim.

Beyond the Moon & Stars

MARY JANE DODD

Accent braided linen with copper heishi and silver cubes in this unique necklace.

we are star stuff.

jr. carl sagan

MATERIALS

4 ivory-and-teal 8mm lampwork rounds

1 copper 20x42mm stamped rectangle pendant

3 hill tribe silver 2mm stamped cubes

10 copper 4mm heishi

2 copper 2-to-1 hammered connectors

1 aqua 35mm moon porcelain pendant

1 copper 10x20mm double-hook clasp

8 copper 7mm bead caps

4" of copper 5x12mm unsoldered twisted curb chain

9" of dark chocolate 3-ply Irish waxed linen

16" of teal 3-ply Irish waxed linen

32" of olive drab 3-ply Irish waxed linen

14" of dark brown 2mm leather cord

3" of sterling silver 24-gauge wire

6" of copper 24-gauge wire

6" of sterling silver 22-gauge wire

3" of sterling silver 20-gauge wire

6" of copper 20-gauge wire

Fabric glue

TOOLS

2 pairs of chain- or flat-nose pliers

Round-nose pliers

Wire cutters

Scissors

Ruler

2 clothespins or binder clips

TECHNIQUES

Square knot, page 26

Lark's head knot, page 26

Wire wrapping, page 25

Wrapped loop, page 23

Braiding, page 27

Overhand knot, page 26

FINISHED SIZE

17"

1 Use 3" of 20-gauge copper wire to form a wrapped loop that attaches to the right loop of the copper pendant.

2 String 1 bead cap, 1 lampwork round, and 1 bead cap; form a wrapped loop.

3 Use 3" of 20-gauge copper wire to form a wrapped loop that attaches to the previous wrapped loop. Repeat Step 2. Use 3" of 20-gauge sterling silver wire to form a wrapped loop that attaches to the previous wrapped loop. Repeat Step 2. Use the single loop of the copper connector to string the previous wrapped loop. Use 3" of 22-gauge sterling silver wire to wrap the two loops of the copper connector closed. Repeat with other copper connector.

4 Use 7" of leather to string one of the two free loops on the connector. Fold the leather 5/8" from the end against itself. Clamp. Repeat entire step with other cord.

5 Remove clamps. Dab glue in the folds of the cords. Use 3" of 24-gauge copper wire to wrap cords together. Repeat entire step with other ends of cords and remaining connector.

6 Use 3" of chocolate linen to form a lark's head knot on the previous copper connector. Use both cords to string 1 bead cap, 1 lampwork round, and 1 bead cap. Use both cords to form an overhand knot. Trim ends unevenly.

7 Center the loop on the left side of the pendant on two 16" olive linen cirds and one 16" teal cord. Divide the cords into three groups of mixed colors.

8 Braid for 1/8". Use 2 cords to string 1 heishi. Use 2 other cords to string 1 heishi on the opposite side of the braid. Braid for 1/8". Use 2 cords to string 1 silver cube in the middle of the braid. Repeat entire step four times, omitting the last 2 silver cubes.

9 Use all six cords to string 1 link on one end of the chain. Fold the linen 1/2" from the ends. Use the 24-gauge sterling silver to wrap the cord ends. Use 3" of chocolate linen to form a square knot over the wire. Trim.

10 Attach the other end of the chain to the hook clasp, opening and closing the chain link as you would a jump ring.

11 Use 3" of chocolate linen to string the moon pendant from the bottom hole of the copper pendant. Form a square knot. Trim.

The Gardener

LORELEI EURTO

The rich green, rust, and blue
hues of this embroidered ribbon
inspired this springtime bracelet.

MATERIALS

2 brown 18mm ceramic rings

1 blue 12mm plastic 4-holed button

1 gold 14mm plastic 2-holed button

1 brown 20mm Bakelite 2-holed button

1 brass 14x8mm lobster clasp

1 brass 4mm jump ring

2 brass 10mm jump rings

6" (17 links) of brass 10mm round unsoldered chain

9" of green/rust/blue floral 10mm embroidered ribbon

8" of copper 22-gauge wire

TOOLS

Wire cutters

Scissors

2 pairs of chain- or flat-nose pliers

TECHNIQUE

Wire wrapping, page 25

FINISHED SIZE

7¼"

TIP

Folding embroidered ribbon in half hides the less attractive side from sight.

1 String 1 ceramic ring to the center of 4½" of ribbon. Use both ends to string one 10mm jump ring about 1" from the ends. Use 4" of wire to wrap the ribbon ends snug against the jump ring.

2 Disassemble the chain into one 2-link piece, two 3-link pieces, one 4-link piece, and one 5-link piece, opening and closing the links as you would jump rings. Attach one end of the 2-link chain to the ceramic ring. Attach the other end to one hole of the blue button. Use one end of one 3-link chain to attach the opposite hole of the blue button to one hole in the gold button. Use one end of the remaining 3-link chain to attach the other buttonhole of the gold button to the remaining ceramic ring.

3 Use the 4-link chain to attach the first ceramic ring to one hole of the brown button. Use the 5-link chain to attach the other buttonhole to the second ceramic ring. Repeat Step 1 with the previous ceramic ring. Use the 4mm jump ring to attach the clasp to the 10mm jump ring.

SUEDE SPIRALS

ERIN SIEGEL

Create suede frames
for rich gemstone
rounds in this earthy
necklace.

MATERIALS

14 agate 12mm rounds

2 green 18mm green ceramic textured spiral coins

1 green 22mm ceramic textured spiral coin

3 copper 4mm cornerless cubes

18 antique copper 7mm corrugated rounds

1 antique copper 16x23mm hammered teardrop toggle clasp

2 copper 2mm crimp tubes

2 copper 3mm crimp covers

33" of tan 5mm suede lace

23" of .019 copper beading wire

TOOLS

Wire cutters

Crimping pliers

Scissors

Ruler

Leather hole punch

TECHNIQUES

Leather hole punching, page 28

Crimp covers, page 22

FINISHED SIZE

17¾"

TIP

Leather or suede lace is ideal for this project since the ends do not fray.

1 Punch one ¹⁄₁₆" hole in the middle of one 2¼" piece of suede lace. Punch one ¹⁄₁₆" hole ⅛" from one end. Repeat for the other end. Repeat entire step thirteen times for a total of 14 suede pieces. Set aside.

2 Use the stringing wire to string 1 crimp tube and the bar half of the clasp; pass back through the tube and crimp. Cover the crimp tube with 1 crimp cover. String 2 cornerless cubes and 1 copper round.

3 *String the center hole of 1 suede piece, 1 agate round, the hole on the left end of the suede, the hole on the right end of the suede, and 1 copper round.** Repeat from * to ** five times. String one 18mm ceramic coin and 1 copper round. Repeat from * to **.

4 String the 22mm ceramic coin and 1 copper round. Repeat Step 3, reversing the stringing sequence. String 1 cornerless cube, 1 crimp tube and the ring half of the clasp; pass back through the tube. Crimp and cover.

SARI SUMMER

TRACY STATLER

Knots in bright sari silk
help keep the silver chain
in place in this sweet
lightweight bracelet.

MATERIALS

1 carnelian 4mm faceted round

1 carnelian 7x5mm faceted rondelle

1 turquoise 8mm heishi

2 green 6mm shell heishi

3 sterling silver 3mm daisy spacers

1 silver 12x30mm S-hook clasp

3 sterling silver 21-gauge head pins

1 silver 6mm jump ring

2 silver 4x10mm fold-over cord ends

12½" of antique silver-plated 14mm unsoldered/10mm soldered round chain

8" of multicolored 30mm sari silk ribbon

Instant adhesive

TOOLS

Scissors

2 pairs of chain- or flat-nose pliers

Round-nose pliers

Wire cutters

Ruler

TECHNIQUES

Wrapped loops, page 23

Overhand knots, page 26

Fold-over cord ends, page 28

FINISHED SIZE

7½"

TIP

Turn soldered chain links into jump rings by cutting them with wire cutters.

1 Use the sari ribbon to form an overhand knot about 1" from one end. *Form an overhand knot about 1" from the previous knot. Repeat from * twice.

2 Dab glue into one cord end and place one end of the ribbon inside. Close with flat-nose pliers. Let dry. Repeat for other end of the ribbon.

3 Use the jump ring to attach the clasp to the cord end. Attach one end of 8" of chain to the clasp. Weave the ribbon through the fourth chain link. Attach the other end of the chain to the cord end.

4 Disassemble the remaining chain and set aside three 10mm links, opening and closing the 14mm links as you would jump rings. Cut the 10mm chain links to create three 10mm jump rings. Use one 10mm jump ring to connect the ribbon to the chain after the seventh chain link. Repeat twice to attach one 10mm jump ring after the tenth and fourteenth chain links.

5 Use 1 head pin to string 1 silver daisy spacer and the 2 green shells. Form a wrapped loop that attaches to the eighth chain link. Use 1 head pin to string 1 silver daisy spacer, the turquoise rondelle, and the carnelian round. Form a wrapped loop that attaches to the 10mm jump ring after the tenth chain link. Use 1 head pin to string 1 silver daisy spacer and the carnelian rondelle. Form a wrapped link that attaches to the tenth link.

SAKURA

ERIN SIEGEL

This delicate necklace
with its braided brown
linen cord and pink coral
dangles resembles a
cherry tree in spring.

MATERIALS

1 pink 5mm top-drilled pearl

7 pink coral 4mm rounds

23 rose quartz 6mm rounds

1 silver 17x13mm Greek ceramic saucer

1 brown-and-pink 25mm ceramic blossom coin

2 sterling silver 5mm daisy spacers

7 sterling silver 2" head pins

1 sterling silver 3" head pin

90" of chocolate brown 4-ply Irish waxed linen cord

6" of sterling silver 24-gauge wire

6" of sterling silver 20-gauge wire

TOOLS

Scissors

Ruler

Tape (optional)

Macramé board and T-pin or clipboard

TECHNIQUES

Double-wrapped loops, page 23

Wrapped-loop bail, page 24

Simple loops, page 23

Overhand knots, page 26

Double overhand knots, page 26

Braiding, page 27

FINISHED SIZE

18"

TIP

A braided-loop closure is not only beautiful but more durable than one that uses a single cord.

1 Use one 2" head pin to string 1 pink coral round; form a double-wrapped loop. Repeat six times to form 7 pink coral dangles. Use the 3" head pin to string 1 rose quartz round; form a double-wrapped loop. Use the 24-gauge wire and the pink pearl to form a wrapped-loop bail and continue wrapping the wire down around the top of the pearl. Set dangles aside.

2 Use the 20-gauge wire to form a simple loop. String 1 daisy spacer, the ceramic blossom coin, and 1 daisy spacer; form a double-wrapped loop. String 1 pink coral dangle, the rose quartz dangle, and the pearl dangle on the simple loop. Set pendant aside.

3 Use three 30" pieces of cord to form a loose overhand knot, leaving a 1" tail. Pin the knot to the macramé board with the T-pin. Braid the 3 cords for 3" and remove from the board. Untie the knot. Fold about 2" of braided cord onto itself. Form an overhand knot, leaving a ½" loop. Pin the loop onto the board.

4 Braid the cords for ½". Use 1 cord to string 1 rose quartz. Repeat entire step seven times.

5 Braid the cords for ¼". Use 1 cord to string 1 pink coral dangle. Braid the cords for ¼". Use 1 cord to string 1 rose quartz round. Repeat entire step twice.

6 String the loop on the pendant. Braid cords for ½". Repeat Step 5 and Step 4, reversing the stringing and braiding sequence for the other half of the necklace.

7 Use all 3 cords to form an overhand knot. Use all 3 cords to string the silver saucer and form a double overhand knot. Trim ends to ¼" and fray.

CHARMED DRAGONFLY

ERIN SIEGEL

Braided satin cord and
hammered copper cones
give this simple bracelet
a refined look.

MATERIALS

1 amethyst 6mm round

1 copper 19mm dragonfly charm

2 antique copper 8mm hammered cones

1 antique copper 12x16mm S-hook clasp with two attached 7mm soldered jump rings

1 antique copper 3" ball-end head pin

1 antique copper 6mm jump ring

36" of rust 3mm satin cord

12" of antiqued copper 22-gauge wire

Fabric glue

TOOLS

Wire cutters

2 pairs of chain- or flat-nose pliers

Round-nose pliers

Macramé board and T-pins or clipboard

Scissors

Ruler

TECHNIQUES

Braiding, page 27

Cones with wire wrapping, page 25

Double-wrapped loops, page 23

Overhand knot, page 26

FINISHED SIZE

7½"

TIP

Using matching colors for the wire, cones, and clasp adds a sophisticated touch to jewelry.

1 Cut the satin cord into three 12" pieces. Use all 3 cords to form a loose overhand knot at one end. Pin the knot to the macramé board. Braid the cords for 6". Dab glue below the previous knot and the end of the braid. Let dry. Remove the braided cord from macramé board. Cut off the overhand knot and the other end of the braid just below the glue.

2 Place the braided cord parallel to the middle of 6" of copper wire. Adjust the braid so that it extends ¼" below the wire. Use one end of the wire to wrap the cord tightly toward the short end of the braid. Use the other wire to string 1 cone; form a double-wrapped loop that attaches to 1 jump ring on the clasp. Repeat entire step for the other end of the braided cord.

3 Use the head pin to string the amethyst round; form a double-wrapped loop that attaches to 1 jump ring on the clasp. Use the 6mm jump ring to attach the dragonfly charm to the previous jump ring.

UNFOLDING

MARY JANE DODD

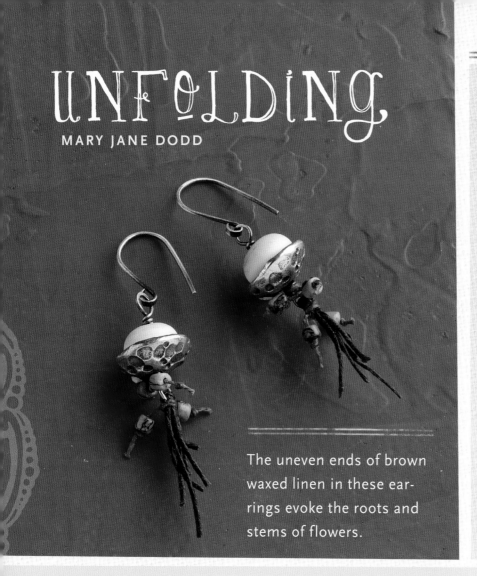

The uneven ends of brown waxed linen in these earrings evoke the roots and stems of flowers.

MATERIALS

2 ivory 10x8mm lampwork rondelles

8 gaspeite 3mm heishi

2 pewter 14mm textured bead caps

2 antiqued sterling silver ear wires

12" of walnut brown 2-ply Irish waxed linen

9" of dark chocolate 3-ply Irish waxed linen

8" of sterling silver 22-gauge wire

Liver of sulfur (optional)

TOOLS

Chain-nose pliers

Round-nose pliers

Wire cutters

Scissors

Ruler

TECHNIQUES

Overhand knot, page 26

Square knot, page 26

Wrapped loops, page 23

FINISHED SIZE

2¼"

TIP

Patina the sterling silver wire with liver of sulfur if you prefer an antiqued look.

1   Use 4" of wire to form a wrapped loop that attaches to 1 ear wire. String 1 ivory rondelle and 1 bead cap (wide end first). Form a wrapped loop.

2   Use 2" of dark chocolate linen to string the bottom wrapped loop. Repeat with 1½" and 1" of dark chocolate linen. Arrange the ends unevenly. Use 3" of dark walnut linen to wrap around all 3 cords twice below the wire loop. Form a square knot, leaving a 1" tail.

3   Use one end of the dark walnut linen to string 1 gaspeite heishi about ⅛" from the previous knot. Form an overhand knot. Trim, leaving a ⅛" tail. Repeat entire step using the other end of the linen.

4   Use 3" of dark walnut linen to wrap around the wirewrapping just below the bead cap. Form a square knot perpendicular to the previous knot. Repeat Step 3.

5   Repeat Steps 1–4 for second earring.

FLYING THROUGH HOOPS

LORELEI EURTO

MATERIALS

2 brass 3mm melon rounds

2 pewter 20x15mm Flying Hearts

2 teal 28mm copper hammered rings

2 brass 2" head pins

2 brass 4mm jump rings

4 brass 7mm jump rings

2 brass 19x27mm ear wires

2½" of brown 5mm deerskin leather lace

TOOLS

Leather punch

2 pairs of chain- or flat-nose pliers

Round-nose pliers

Wire cutters

Scissors

TECHNIQUES

Leather hole punching, page 28

Simple loops, page 23

FINISHED SIZE

2½"

Leather lace adds texture to these lighthearted hoop earrings.

TIP

Punching both holes in the leather at one time is not only quicker but ensures the holes line up perfectly.

1 Use 1 head pin to string 1 melon round and 1 pewter heart (bottom to top). Form a simple loop that attaches to one 7mm jump ring. Set aside.

2 Fold 1¼" piece of leather in half and punch one hole through both pieces ⅛" from the ends. Use the leather to string the previous jump ring. Fold the leather over 1 teal ring and use one 7mm jump ring to string both holes in the leather. Use one 4mm jump ring to attach the previous jump ring to 1 ear wire.

3 Repeat Steps 1–2 for other earring.

THE BEACH HOUSE

LORELEI EURTO

Pretty filigree tubes keep multiple cords corralled in this stunning leather, seed bead, and beaded chain necklace.

MATERIALS

300 matte mint 2x4mm peanut seed beads

6 assorted 8x6mm etched lampwork rondelles in yellow, tan, blue, and green

1 ivory-and-brown 12x15mm lampwork barrel

8 gray 15mm rubber O-rings

2 brass 5x8mm filigree tubes

14 copper 5mm daisy spacers

1 brown 18x35mm ceramic window-and-key toggle clasp

2 brass 7mm jump rings

2 brass 10mm jump rings

2 copper 3mm crimp tubes

2 brass 5x9mm fold-over cord ends

40" of brown 2mm leather cord

15" of brass 20-gauge wire

21" of .018 beading wire

TOOLS

Round-nose pliers

2 pairs of chain- or flat-nose pliers

Crimping pliers

Wire cutters

TECHNIQUES

Fold-over cord ends, page 28

Wrapped loops, page 23

FINISHED SIZE

21"

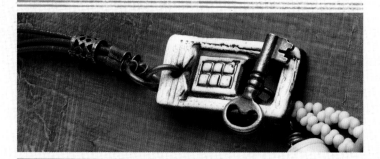

TIP

Contrasting textures and finishes such as shiny, smooth lampwork glass paired with matte, bumpy seed beads ensure that a necklace is fascinating from every angle.

1 Fold two 20" pieces of leather cord in half. Use all four ends to string 2 filigree tubes. Insert two leather ends into one cord end and close. Repeat with remaining two leather ends and cord end. Use one 10mm jump ring to attach both cord ends to one 10mm jump ring. Attach the previous jump ring to the window half of the clasp. Set aside.

2 Use the beading wire to string 1 crimp tube and one 7mm jump ring. Pass back through the crimp tube and crimp. String 300 peanut seed beads. String the 2 leather cords opposite the clasp. String 1 crimp tube and the previous 7mm jump ring; pass back through the crimp tube and crimp. String 2 O-rings over the beaded strand. Use one 7mm jump ring to attach the key half of the clasp to the previous 7mm jump ring.

3 Use 2" of brass wire to form a wrapped loop that attaches to the leather cords opposite the window half of the clasp. String 1 spacer, 1 rondelle, and 1 spacer; form a wrapped loop that attaches to 1 O-ring.

4 Use 2" of brass wire to form a wrapped loop that attaches to the previous O-ring. String 1 spacer, 1 rondelle, and 1 spacer; form a wrapped loop that attaches to 1 O-ring.

5 Use 3" of brass wire to form a wrapped loop that attaches to the previous O-ring. String 1 spacer, the lampwork barrel, and 1 spacer; form a wrapped loop that attaches to 1 O-ring. Repeat Step 4 three times. Use 2" of brass wire to form a wrapped loop that attaches to the previous O-ring. String 1 spacer, 1 rondelle, and 1 spacer; form a wrapped loop that attaches to the 7mm jump ring on the end of the beaded strand.

FLY, LITTLE BIRD

LORELEI EURTO

Rustic letter charms spell
out a bird's deepest wish
in this peaceful bracelet.

MATERIALS

39 periwinkle 5x3mm African glass rondelles (A)

1 aqua 5x7mm etched glass barrel (B)

1 pale blue 5x7mm faceted glass rondelle (C)

2 mint 8mm recycled glass barrels (D)

1 blue 8mm vintage glass round (E)

2 blue 8mm Picasso faceted pressed-glass rounds (F)

1 teal 11x20mm pressed-glass rectangle (G)

6 golden pyrite 3mm faceted rounds (H)

1 turquoise 8mm faceted round (J)

2 teal jade 8mm faceted rounds (K)

1 amazonite 15x10mm faceted nugget (L)

1 tan-and-brown 10x12mm ceramic "F" charm

1 tan-and-brown 10x12mm ceramic "L" charm

1 tan-and-brown 10x12mm ceramic "Y" charm

1 shibuichi 48x20mm bird hook-and-eye clasp

5 brass 3mm jump rings

2 silver 3mm crimp tubes

6" of copper 8mm round link chain

10" of blue 4-ply waxed linen cord

10" of light green 2mm silk cord

10" of green 4-ply waxed linen cord

TOOLS

Crimping pliers

Wire cutters

Scissors

TECHNIQUE

Overhand knot, page 26

FINISHED SIZE

7¾"

TIP

Match your cord to bead colors for an understated look.

1 Attach 1 jump ring to 1 ceramic charm. Repeat twice. Set aside.

2 Use the blue cord to string 1A, leaving a 2" tail. Form an overhand knot. String 1A and form an overhand knot. Repeat thirty-seven times. Set aside.

3 Use the green cord to string 1L, leaving a 2" tail. Form an overhand knot. String the following beads, forming an overhand knot in between each one: 1F, 1K, 1G, 1B, 1D, 1E, 1C, 1H, the F charm, 2H, the L charm, 2H, the Y charm, 1 H, 1D, 1J, 1K, 1F. Set aside.

4 *Use the end of the strands created in Steps 1 and 2 and the green silk cord to form an overhand knot. Use all 3 strands to string 1 crimp tube and the bird half of the clasp. Pass back through the crimp tube and crimp. Trim. Use 1 jump ring to attach one end of the chain to all 3 cords below the knot.** Weave the silk cord through the chain. Repeat from * to * for the other half of the bracelet, using the wing half of the clasp.

AFTERNOON TEA

Silk ribbon: Marsha Neal Studio. *Ceramic beads:* NKP Designs. *Wire:* Patina Queen. *Jump rings and crystals:* Fire Mountain Gems and Beads. *Head pins:* Miss Fickle Media. *All other materials:* The Riverwalk Bead Shop and Gallery.

AUTUMNAL ARRANGEMENT

Discs: Z Designs in Glass. *Rondelles:* Pinocean. *Pixies:* MyElements. *Washers:* Elaine Ray (Ornamentea). *Silk cord:* FusionBeads.com. *Spacers:* Bead Breakout. *Brass chain and findings:* Vintaj Natural Brass Co.

AWAKENING LOTUS

Brass link: Brass Bouquet. *Ivory and small sage rondelles:* Pinocean. *Purple and large sage rondelles:* Patty Lakinsmith. *Brass beads:* Sharon Unlimited. *Brass jump rings:* Beadaholique. *Irish waxed linen:* Karleigh Jae. *Leather cord:* Artbeads.com. *Brass wire:* The Birds and the Beads. *Fabri-Tac:* Michaels.

BATIK BOUTIQUE

Button: Summers Studio. *Wood beads:* Bead Master USA. *Findings:* Vintaj Natural Brass Co. *Wire:* Patina Queen. *Ribbon:* Class Act Designs. *C-Lon 400 cord:* Bello Modo.

THE BEACH HOUSE

Rondelles: Mermaid Glass. *Toggle:* Earthenwood Studio. *Barrel:* Melissa Rediger. *O-rings:* MyElements. *Seed beads:* FusionBeads.com. *Findings and filigree beads:* Vintaj Natural Brass Co. *Cord:* Beads and Pieces.

BEYOND THE MOON AND STARS

Pendant: Spirited Earth. *Lampwork beads:* Pinocean. *Heishi:* Happy Mango Beads. *Cubes, chain, clasp:* Beadaholique. *Cord:* Wild About Pearls. *Linen:* Karleigh Jae. *Silver wire:* Monsterslayer. *All other materials:* Speaking Your Truth.

BLACK FLOWERS

Leather cord: Leather Cord USA. *Flower barrels and G-S Hypo Cement:* Michaels. *All other materials:* Fire Mountain Gems and Beads.

BOHEMIAN WRAPSODY

Ribbon: Beadaholique. *Shell:* Beadazzled. *All other materials:* Fire Mountain Gems and Beads.

BUTTERFLY SONG

Pendant: Yolanda's Clay. *Ceramic mermaid rounds:* Gaea. *Leather:* Leather Cord USA. *Jump rings:* FusionBeads.com. *Wood beads:* Walmart. *Seed beads:* Micheals. *Turquoise and crimp ends:* Artbeads.com. *All other materials:* The Riverwalk Bead Shop and Gallery.

CAREY

Brass findings: Vintaj Natural Brass Co. *Pendant:* Gaea Beads. *Gemstones:* Rings & Things. *Ribbon:* Michaels.

CHARMED DRAGONFLY

Charm: Summers Studio. *Satin cord:* Bello Modo. *Wire:* Patina Queen. *Head pin:* Miss Fickle Media. *All other materials:* Artbeads.com.

COPPER ANTIQUITY

Cord: Bello Modo. *Washers and ear wires:* Miss Fickle Media. *Turquoise:* The Riverwalk Bead Shop and Gallery.

CROON

Leather cord: Leather Cord USA. *Similar pendant:* More Skye Jewels. *Ceramic melon rounds:* CGP Gem Beads. *Red rounds:* Michaels. *Jump ring:* Vintaj Natural Brass Co.

DAISY CUFF

Ceramic beads: Golem Studio. *Rubber O-rings:* MyElements. *Brass spacers:* Hands of the Hills. *Leather lace:* Ornamentea.

DELICATE THINGS

Ceramic donut: Becky Guzman. *S-clasp and knot cups:* The Riverwalk Bead Shop and Gallery. *All other materials:* Artbeads.com.

ECLECTIC ERIN

Industrial Chic clasp and link and all other materials: Michaels.

ELEMENTS OF EARTH

Wood rounds and silver ovals: Michaels. *Raku beads:* Elements Pottery. *Agate:* The Riverwalk Bead Shop and Gallery. *Seed beads:* FusionBeads.com. *Button:* Jo-Ann Fabrics & Crafts. *Cord:* Bello Modo.

FLEUR-DE-LIS

All materials: Michaels.

FLIRTATION LARIAT

Ribbon: Lima Beads. *Ribbon ends:* Ornamentea. *Swarovski crystals and similar pearls:* FusionBeads.com. *Findings:* Vintaj Natural Brass Co. *Chain:* Michaels.

FLYING THROUGH HOOPS

Hearts: Green Girl Studios. *Hoops:* Miss Fickle Media. *Leather:* Ornamentea. *Findings:* Vintaj Natural Brass Co.

FLY, LITTLE BIRD

Clasp: Green Girl Studios. *Charms:* Elaine Ray (Ornamentea). *African glass beads:* Hands of the Hills. *Recycled glass beads:* Happy Mango Beads. *Brass findings:* Vintaj Natural Brass Co. *Chain:* Primitive Earth Beads and Chain. *Cord:* Bello Modo. *Beadalon crimp tubes:* Michaels. *Similar glass and stones:* Lima Beads.

THE GARDENER

Buttons: Black Sheep Yarns. *Ribbon:* Tinsel Trading Co. *Ceramic rings:* Round Rabbit Extra. *Wire:* Patina Queen. *Jump rings, clasp, and chain:* Vintaj Natural Brass Co.

GARDEN GRACES

Charm: Mary Harding. *Swarovski crystals:* Michaels. *Briolettes:* Beads and Pieces. *Brass cubes and spacer:* Hands of the Hills. *Wire:* Patina Queen. *Silk cord and similar glass beads:* FusionBeads.com. *Brass findings:* Vintaj Natural Brass Co.

HOME IS WHERE THE HEART IS

House: Diane Hawkey. *Heart:* Lynn Davis. *Button:* Meluna Beads. *Cord:* FusionBeads.com. *Rings:* Objects and Elements.

HOW DOES YOUR GARDEN GROW?

Pendant: Earthenwood Studio. *"Grow" bead:* Diane Hawkey. *Toggle:* Green Girl Studios. *Enameled flowers:* C-Koop Beads. *Beadalon crimps:* Michaels. *Beading wire:* Soft Flex Co. *Brass wire:* Patina Queen. *Rust seed beads:* Jo-Ann Fabrics & Crafts. *Tubes and jump rings:* Vintaj Natural Brass Co. *All other materials:* FusionBeads.com.

INDIGO FOREST

Wood triangles: Michaels. *Wood rounds:* Jo-Ann Fabrics & Crafts. *Ceramic beads and pendant:* Yolanda's Clay. *Cord:* The Bead Gallery. *Clasp:* Artbeads.com. *All other materials:* The Riverwalk Bead Shop and Gallery.

IN THE GARDEN

Pendant: Micic Art. *Ribbon:* Marsha Neal Studio. *All other materials:* Artbeads.com.

LAVENDER

Buttons: Mamacita Beadworks. *Ribbon:* Marsha Neal Studio. *Wire:* Patina Queen. *Ear wires:* Vintaj Natural Brass Co.

LEATHER RUFFLE HOOPS

Hoops: Miss Fickle Media. *All other materials:* Ornamentea.

MY AFFECTION

Pendant: Eri Pottery. *Disc:* Marsha Neal Studio. *Chain:* Rings & Things. *Douppioni silk:* Angela Brittain. *Fairy silk:* Bello Modo. *Brass findings:* Vintaj Natural Brass Co.

NOUVELLE

Findings: Vintaj Natural Brass Co. *Agate:* CGP Gem Beads. *Sari silk:* Brea Bead Works.

OCEAN LOVE

"Ocean Love" silk cord set: Marsha Neal Studio. *Linen cord:* Ornamentea. *Glass rounds:* Happy Mango Beads. *Clasp:* Rings & Things. *Ceramic round:* Lisa Peters Art. *Brass rounds and jump rings:* Vintaj Natural Brass Co.

OXFORD CIRCUS

Link: Amanda Davie. *Ribbon ends:* Ornamentea. *Ribbon:* V.V. Rouleaux. *Coin:* Reduction Nation. *All other materials:* Vintaj Natural Brass Co.

PEARLY YOURS

Pendant: Jade Scott. *Similar glass flower:* FusionBeads.com. *Button:* Black Sheep Yarns. *Chain and Head pin:* Vintaj Natural Brass Co. *Silk ribbon:* Bello Modo.

POMPIDOU

Linen cord: Bello Modo. *All other materials:* Michaels.

QUEEN ANNE'S LACE

Pendant: Golem Studios. *Leather:* Happy Mango Beads. *Similar lace:* Moment of Nostalgia. *Silk and Griffin cord:* FusionBeads.com. *Jump rings:* Bead Center. *Similar chain:* AD Adornments.

QUIETUDE

Discs: Alora Beads. *Pendant:* Swoon Dimples. *Link:* Green Girl Studios. *Button:* Tierra Cast. *Cord:* FusionBeads.com. *Hook clasp:* Vintaj Natural Brass Co. *Chain:* Lima Beads. *Heart:* Gaea.

RAKU RIBBONS

Ribbon yarn: Bello Modo. *Pendant:* Southern Fired Designs. *Mauve, gray, and red ceramic rounds:* Jon Sutcliffe. *Red raku (10mm) ceramic rounds:* Sedillo Hill Studio. *Cones:* Bead Creative. *Head pins:* Miss Fickle Media. *All other materials:* The Riverwalk Bead Shop and Gallery.

SAKURA

Coin: Summers Studio. *Saucer:* Fire and Fibers. *Cord:* Bello Modo. *Coral:* Michaels. *All other materials:* The Riverwalk Bead Shop and Gallery.

SARI SUMMER

Sari ribbon: Darn Good Yarn. *Clasp and G-S Hypo Cement:* Michaels. *Gemstones and shell:* Znet Shows. *All other materials:* Fire Mountain Gems and Beads.

SHIMMERING PEARLS

Jump rings and head pin: Beadaholique. *Clasp:* Bello Modo. *All other materials:* Michaels.

SIMPLY PEACEFUL

Carnelian: Artbeads.com. *Pendant:* Seoul Identity. *Clasp and head pin:* Miss Fickle Media. *All other materials:* The Riverwalk Bead Shop and Gallery.

SONORAN SUNSET

Deerskin lace: Leather Cord USA. *Copper links:* Cherry Tree Beads. *Agate and glass:* Artbeads.com.

SOUL SISTER

Bangle: Artbeads.com. *Lampwork beads:* Kelley's Beads. *Cord:* Fire Mountain Gems and Beads. *Copper rounds:* The Riverwalk Bead Shop and Gallery. *Ribbon:* Bello Modo.

SUEDE SPIRALS

Ceramic beads: Vanessa Gilkes. *Agate:* Bead Creative. *Suede:* Leather Cord USA. *Copper cubes:* Bead Gallery. *All other materials:* The Riverwalk Bead Shop and Gallery.

SWEET NECTAR

Pendant: Hint Jewelry. *Tube:* Lisa Peters Art. *Similar Bakelite button:* Black Sheep Yarns. *Silver button:* Tierra Cast. *Brass wire:* Patina Queen. *Cord:* Ornamentea. *Silver wire:* Shipwreck Beads.

TIDY TRIMMINGS

Sugared and brass Lucite: City Beads. *Pink Lucite round:* Reduction Nation. *Trim:* Tinsel Trading Co. *Findings:* Vintaj Natural Brass Co. *Brass wire:* Patina Queen. *Beading wire:* Soft Flex Co. *Beadalon crimp tubes:* Michaels. *Jade rondelles:* Lima Beads.

TRIPLE LOOP

Cord: Ornamentea. *Amethyst and glass:* Fire Mountain Gems and Beads. *All other materials:* Beadaholique.

UNFOLDING

Rondelles: Pinocean. *Bead caps:* Mamacita Beadworks. *Irish waxed linen:* Kayleigh Jae. *Gaspeite:* The Birds and The Beads. *Ear wires:* Rocki's Artisan Metalwork & Supplies. *Wire:* Monsterslayer.

VINTAGE GLAM

Sequins: Tinsel Trading Co. *Silk cord:* Artbeads .com. *Washers:* Beadaholique. *Ear wires:* Miss Fickle Media.

WITCH HAZEL

Silk cord: FusionBeads.com. *All other materials:* Michaels.

WHERE TO SHOP

Check your local bead shop or contact:

AD Adornments
adadornments.com

Alora Beads
alorabeads.etsy.com

Angela Brittain
angelabrittain.etsy.com

Artbeads.com
11901 137th Ave. Ct. KPN
Gig Harbor, WA 98329
(866) 715-BEAD (2323)
artbeads.com

Bead Breakout
2314 Monroe Ave.
Brighton, NY 14618
(585) 271-2340
beadbreakout.com

Bead Center
989 Sixth Ave.
New York, NY 10018-0792
(212) 279-2323
beadcenterny.com

Bead Creative
1 Lafayette Rd.
Hampton, NH 03842
(603) 926-8844
nhbeadstore.com

Bead Gallery Inc.
520 Franklin St.
Melrose, MA 02176
(781) 665-0400
beadgalleryinc.com

Bead Master USA (Wholesale only)
beadmasterusa.com

Beadaholique
beadaholique.com

Beadazzled
Tyson Corner Center 1
1961 Chain Bridge Rd.
McLean, VA 22102
(703) 848-2323
wbeadazzled.net

Beads and Pieces
1320 Commerce St., Ste. C
Petaluma, CA 94954
(800) 65-BEADS
beadsandpieces.com

Becky Guzman
Diakonos Designs LLC
187 East Main St.
Stoughton, WI 53589
(608) 575-5642
diakonosdesigns.com

Bello Modo
4826 Libby Rd. NE
Olympia, WA 98506
(360) 357-3443
bellomodo.com

Birds and the Beads, The
411 Rt. 79
Morganville, NJ 07751
(732) 591-8233
thebirdsandthebeads.com

Black Sheep Yarns
blacksheepyarns.etsy.com

Brass Bouquet
(503) 356-1505
brassbouquet.com

Brea Beadworks
1027 E. Imperial Hwy. Ste. D5
Brea, CA 92821
(714) 671-9976
breabeadworks.com

CGP Gem Beads
cgpgembeads.etsy.com

Cherry Tree Beads (Wholesale only)
(828) 505-2328
cherrytreebeads.com

City Beads
15 West 37 St.
New York, NY 10018
(212) 575-1177

C-Koop Beads
2159 Shilhon Rd.
Duluth, MN 55804
(218) 525-7333
ckoopbeads.com

Class Act Designs
6520 Platt Ave. #605
West Hills, CA 91307
classactdesigns.com

Darn Good Yarn
(609) 276-7489
darngoodyarn.com

Diane Hawkey
dianehawkey.com

Earthenwood Studio
PO Box 20002
Ferndale, MI 48220
(248) 548-4793
eathenwoodstudio.com

Elements Pottery
(810) 982-2138
elementspottery.com

Eri Pottery
eripottery.etsy.com

Fire and Fibers
fireandfibers.com

Fire Mountain Gems and Beads
1 Fire Mountain Wy.
Grants Pass, OR 97526
(800) 355-2137
firemountaingems.com

Fusion Beads
3830 Stone Way N.
Seattle, WA 98103
(888) 781-3559
fusionbeads.com

Gaea
PO Box 684
Ojai, CA 93023
(805) 640-8989
gaea.cc

Golem Studio
golemstudio.com

Green Girl Studios
PO Box 19389
Ashevelle, NC 28815
greengirlstudios.com

Hands of the Hills
7432 SE 27th St.
Mercer Island, WA 98040
(206) 232-4588
hohbead.com

Happy Mango Beads
PO Box 64
Berthoud, CO 80513
(970) 532-2546
happymangobeads.com

Hint Jewelry
hint.etsy.com

Jade Scott
jadescott.etsy.com

Jo-Ann Fabric and Craft
joann.com

Jon Sutcliffe
c/o Diakonos Designs LLC
187 East Main St.
Stoughton, WI 53589
(608) 575-5642
diakonosdesigns.com

Karleigh Jae
karleighjae.etsy.com

Kelley's Beads
kelleysbeads.etsy.com

Leather Cord USA
509 Hickory Ridge Trl.
Ste. 110
Woodstock, GA 30188
(877) 700-2673
leathercordusa.com

Lima Beads
limabeads.com

Lisa Peters Art
(201) 784-0812
lisapetersart.com

Lynn Davis
lynndavis.etsy.com

Mamacita Beadworks
mamacitabeadworks.etsy.com

Mary Harding Jewelry
maryhardingjewelry.com

Marsha Neal Studio
PO Box 1560
Hockessin, DE 19707
marshanealstudio.com

Melissa Rediger
mjrbeads.com

Meluna Beads
meluna.etsy.com

Mermaid Glass
mermaidglass.etsy.com

Michaels
michaels.com

Micic Art
micicarts.blogspot.com

Miss Fickle Media
missficklemedia.etsy.com

Moment of Nostalgia
momentofnostalgia.etsy.com

Monsterslayer Inc.
PO Box 550
Kirtland, NM 87417
(505) 598-5322
monsterslayer.com

More Skye Jewels
moreskyejewels.etsy.com

MyElements
myelements.etsy.com

NKP Designs
nkpdesigns.com

Objects and Elements
16128 Old Snohomish-Monroe Rd.
Snohomish, WA 98290
(206) 965-0373
objectsandelements.com

Ornamentea
509 N. West St.
Raleigh, NC 27603
(919) 834-6260
ornamentea.com

Patina Queen
patinaqueen.com

Patty Lakinsmith
playswithfiredesigns.com

Pinocean
pinocean.etsy.com

Primitive Earth Beads
5217 8th Ave. S.
Gulfport, FL 33707
(800) 777-0038
primitiveearthbeads.com

Reduction Nation
reductionnation.etsy.com

Rings & Things
(Wholesale only)
PO Box 450
Spokane, WA 99210
(800) 366-2156
rings-things-com

Riverwalk Bead Shop
and Gallery, The
32 Elm St.
Amesbury, MA 01913
(978) 388-3499
riverwalkbeads.com

Rocki's Artisan Metalwork
& Supplies
rockissupplies.etsy.com

Round Rabbit Extra
roundrabbitextra.bigcartel.com

Sedillo Hill Studio
sedillohillstudio.com

Seoul Identity
(541) 554-7507
seoulidentity.com

Sharon Unlimited
(928) 443-7446
sharonunlimited.com

Shipwreck Beads
8560 Commerce Place Dr. NE
Lacey, WA 98516
(800) 950-4232
shipwreckbeads.com

Soft Flex Company
softflexcompany.com

Southern Fired Designs
240 Riverview Trl.
Roswell, GA 30075
southernfireddesigns.com

Speaking Your Truth
speakingyourtruth.etsy.com

Spirited Earth
spiritedearth.etsy.com

Summers Studio
summersstudioetc.etsy.com

Swoon Dimples
swoondimples.etsy.com

Tierra Cast
(Wholesale only)
3177 Guerneville Rd.
Santa Rosa, CA 95401
(800) 222-9939
tierracast.com

Tinsel Trading Co.
1 West 37th St.
New York, NY 10018
(212) 730-1030
tinseltrading.com

Vanessa Gilkes
culturezine.com

Vintaj Natural Brass Co.
(Wholesale only)
PO Box 246
Galena, IL 61036
vintaj.com

V.V. Rouleaux
261 Pavilion Rd.
Sloane Square
Kensington SW1X 0PB
United Kingdom
vvrouleaux.com

Walmart
walmart.com

Wild About Pearls
wildaboutpearls.etsy.com

Yolanda's Clay
yolandasclay.etsy.com

Z Designs in Glass
zdesigns@hotmail.com

Znet Shows Inc.
(Wholesale only)
7 Executive Park Ct.
Germantown, MD 20874
(866) 824-1832
znetshows.com

This chart includes approximate metric conversions for measurements up to 24" (61 cm). For measurements not listed here, or for precise conversions, use a ruler, tape measure, or online conversion guide such as onlineconversion.com.

Inches	Centimeters	Inches	Centimeters	Inches	Centimeters
1/16	.02	6½	16.5	16	40.5
1/8	.03	7	18	16½	42
1/4	.06	7½	19	17	43
3/8	1	8	20.5	17½	44.5
1/2	1.3	8½	21.5	18	45.5
5/8	1.5	9	23	18½	47
3/4	2	9½	24	19	48.5
7/8	2.2	10	25.5	19½	49.5
1	2.5	10½	26.5	20	51
1½	3.8	11	28	20½	52
2	5	11½	29	21	53.5
2½	6.5	12	30.5	21½	54.5
3	7.5	12½	31.5	22	56
3½	9	13	33	22½	57
4	10	13½	34.5	23	58.5
4½	11.5	14	35.5	23½	59.5
5	12.5	14½	37	24	61
5½	14	15	38		
6	15	15½	39.5		

CONTRIBUTORS

MEET THE AUTHORS

Erin Siegel
erinsiegel.com

Erin is an accomplished jewelry designer and beading instructor with a passion for sharing her knowledge, experience, and ideas. She loves creating casual, everyday jewelry with rustic, organic materials such as antiqued metals, gemstones, and waxed linen cord. Her jewelry projects have been published in *Stringing* and *Bead Trends*. Erin lives in Massachusetts with her husband, Josh, and daughter, Nora.

Lorelei Eurto
loreleieurtojewelry.etsy.com

Lorelei is a prolific self-taught jewelry designer with a successful online jewelry business and a popular jewelry blog. She loves adding unique textural elements to her jewelry and showcasing her love of art beads in her fun and easy-to-wear designs. Her jewelry has been published in *Stringing*, *BeadStyle*, *Bead Trends*, *Step by Step Beads* and *Creative Jewelry*, plus the books *Chain Style* and *Wire Style 2*. Lorelei lives in New York State with her husband, Joe.

MEET THE CONTRIBUTORS

Mary Jane Dodd
mairedodd.blogspot.com

Mary Jane has been creating personal adornment for more than twelve years and enjoys finding the threads that connect the personal to the universal. Her designs have appeared in *Belle Armoire Jewelry* and *Step by Step Wire Jewelry*, as well as in juried exhibits, including a 2010 show at the Newark Museum. A member of the New Jersey Metal Arts Guild, Mary Jane lives in Neptune, New Jersey, with her three children.

Denise Yezbak Moore
rustyroxx.etsy.com

Denise is a self-taught artisan who works as a freelance jewelry designer for Halcraft USA. Her designs have been frequently published. She often includes semiprecious gemstones, vintage glass, artisan pendants, lampwork beads, and Swarovski crystals in her romantic and whimsical designs. Denise lives in Orange County, California, with her husband, Rusty, son, Garrett, and daughter, Britton.

Tracy Statler
makebraceletsblog.com

Tracy is a self-taught jewelry designer who began making jewelry more than eight years ago. She enjoys making stylish and comfortable pieces with natural elements such as gemstones, wood beads, and soft stringing materials. Bracelets are her favorite type of jewelry to make. Tracy lives in northern Virginia with her husband, Patrick, son, Nicholas; and daughter, Brinn.

INDEX

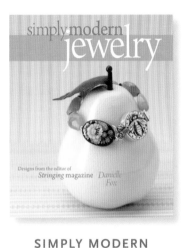